Knitting
for the first time®

Knitting
for the first time™

Vanessa-Ann

Sterling Publishing Co., Inc.
New York
A Sterling/Chapelle Book

Chapelle Ltd.

Jo Packham
Sara Toliver
Cindy Stoeckl

Editor: Leslie Farmer
Technical Advisor: Geraldine Ridenour
Graphic Illustrator: Kim Taylor
Photography: Kevin Dilley for Hazen Photography
Photo Stylist: Jill Dahlberg
Editorial Director: Caroll Shreeve
Art Director: Karla Haberstich
Copy Editor: Marilyn Goff
Staff: Burgundy Alleman, Areta Bingham, Ray Cornia,
Emily Frandsen, Susan Jorgensen, Barbara Milburn, Lecia Monsen,
Karmen Quinney, Desirée Wybrow

Models: Savanna Ball, Allie Dixon, Natalie Dixon, Tonnie Dixon,
Sydney Fowers, Jenna Hall, Meili Hall, Jordynn Mitchell,
Jayden Wybrow

Library of Congress Cataloging-in-Publication Data Available

Knitting for the first time.
    p. cm.
"A Sterling/Chapelle Book."
  ISBN 0-8069-6415-4
  1. Knitting. 2. Knitting--Patterns.
TT820.K6987 2003
746.43'2--dc21

                        2002155103

10 9 8 7 6 5 4 3 2 1

Published by Sterling Publishing Co., Inc.
387 Park Avenue South, New York, NY 10016
©2003 by Chapelle Ltd.
Distributed in Canada by Sterling Publishing
c/o Canadian Manda Group, One Atlantic Avenue, Suite 105
Toronto, Ontario, Canada M6K 3E7
Distributed in Great Britain by Chrysalis Books
64 Brewery Road, London N7 9NT, England
Distributed in Australia by Capricorn Link (Australia) Pty. Ltd.
P.O. Box 704, Windsor, NSW 2756, Australia

Sterling ISBN 0-8069-6415-4

Write Us

If you have any questions or comments, please contact:
Chapelle, Ltd., Inc.,
P.O. Box 9252, Ogden, UT 84409
(801) 621-2777 • (801) 621-2788 Fax
e-mail: chapelle@chapelleltd.com
web site: chapelleltd.com

Table of Contents

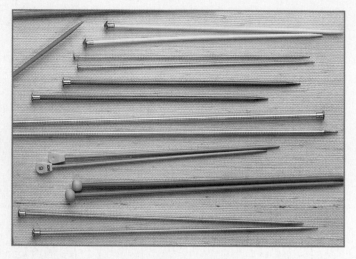

Section 1:

Knitting Basics—10

Section 2:

Basic Techniques—38

Section 3:

Beyond the Basics—78

Section 4:

The Gallery—100

designed by Colinette Yarns, Ltd.

Introduction

Knitting has a history that is as rich and intricate as the woven patterns that are created with its various techniques. As a craft, knitting has been dated back to the Middle Ages. It was a major industry in Europe in the 1500s. It has been *so* prevalent at times in day-to-day life that some of the great fictional writers, such as Charles Dickens in *A Tale of Two Cities*, have chosen to not only make mention the pastime, but to develop a character around it.

Learning to knit is like learning a new language. At first glance, it seems daunting; but if you take it one step at a time, you will find it to be a fun and relaxing activity. First, you begin with the basics—the foundations for being able to form the words, or the patterns. All over the world, we begin our speech patterns as babies with "ma ma" and "da da." In knitting we begin with "knit" and "purl" and build on these two fundamentals. Just as with language, we make the connections between what we have already learned and how it applies to the technique at hand. Soon, we are linking together an entire network of possible patterns.

You will find that knitting also has different "dialects" depending on where you go in the world. There are often many methods for accomplishing the same knitting technique. Sometimes the method is the same, but the term it is given may be slightly different from one region to the next. Some knitters like to knit and hold the yarn in their right hand, while others prefer working with it in their left hand. In Europe, many knitters use a sheath to help hold the knitting needles during the work. Generally, there is no right or wrong to how you knit. It is simply a matter of what feels most comfortable and what works best for you.

Knitting is very versatile and endless in possibilities for creating a unique piece. There is an almost unlimited variety of yarns from which to choose. There are all sizes of knitting needles and stitch patterns that can be used in your piece.

How to use this book

Knitting for the first time™ is divided into four sections. Section 1: Knitting Basics provides basic information about the supplies, materials, and general techniques used in knitting.

In Section 2: Basic Techniques, you will learn the basic stitches, knit and purl, and some of the different ways of manipulating these stitches as well as some of the ways possible for increasing and decreasing the stitches for creating different shapes and patterns to make several beginner to intermediate level projects.

Highlighted text will alert you to a new technique that you will need to learn. The method for completing the new technique will follow the step you are working on, standing alone in a colored box either on the same page or the following page. In subsequent projects, you will be refered back to the method by its name.

Section 3: Beyond the Basics continues with more advanced projects designed to stretch the newly aquired skills of the knitter.

Finally, Section 4: The Gallery presents a showcase of knit artists and their various pieces to woo and wow the new knitter.

The projects herein have been selected with the first-time knitter in mind, teaching you the most basic

stitches and methods for knitting. This book is not a comprehensive volume on knitting by any means—there are simply too many stitch patterns and techniques that could not be addressed due to the limited amount of space.

Just as a travel guide gives you language fundamentals for a journey to a foreign country, we aim to give you a basis for "conversational" knitting and hope that you will seek out more information and become "fluent" by and by.

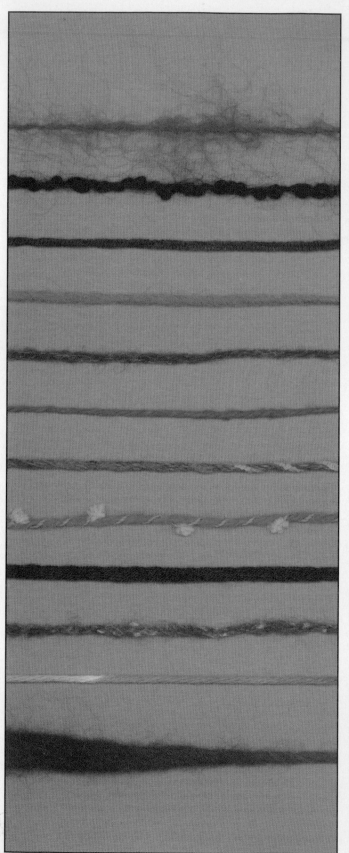

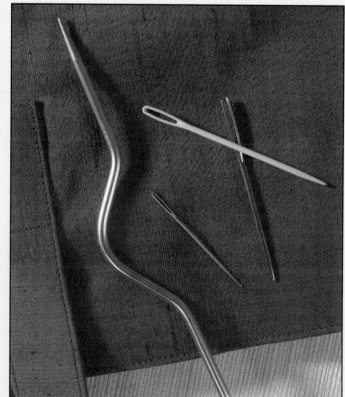

Section 1: knitting basics

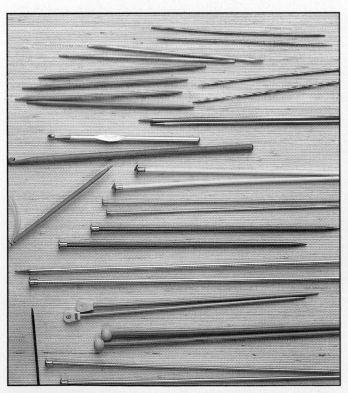

What do I need to get started?

Knitting Needles

The variety of knitting begins with the needles you select for working your piece. Knitting needles come in different shapes, sizes, lengths, and materials to suit your project, your tastes, and your knitting style. (See Photo A)

Needle Shapes

Knitting needles are available in three basic shapes. The first and probably most commonly used shape is the straight needle. Straight needles have a "stop" at one end and a tapered tip at the other. They are the same diameter from just beyond the tip to the stop. These needles are used for traditional "flat" knitting in which the work moves from one needle to the other.

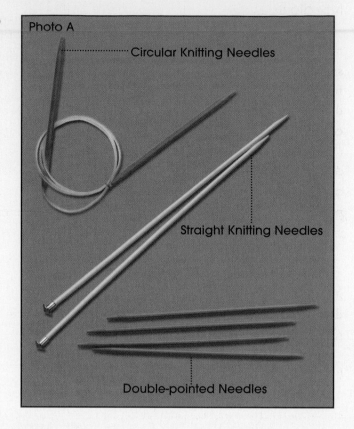
Photo A
Circular Knitting Needles
Straight Knitting Needles
Double-pointed Needles

The next needle shape is the circular needle. Circular needles consist of two needle ends that are wood or metal with a flexible nylon strand between the two ends. They can be used for knitting "in the round" to create a tube shape (a project without a seam) or for flat knitting when you want to keep the center of gravity in your lap instead of at the end of one needle. (See Fig. 1 and Fig. 2)

The third needle shape is the double-pointed needle. Double-pointed needles are straight and have, as their name implies, a point or tip at each end. They come in sets of four or five needles and are also used for knitting a tube shape, but on a smaller scale such as for socks or small sleeves. The stitches are divided evenly between three or four of the needles and the last needle is used for knitting. (See Fig. 3)

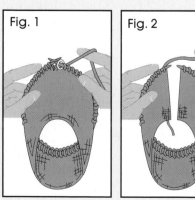
Fig. 1
Fig. 2

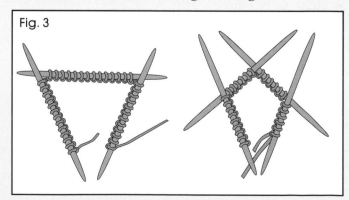
Fig. 3

Needle Sizes

Knitting needles are sized by diameter. The smaller the needle number, the smaller the needle is in diameter and the smaller and tighter the stitch. American sizing of needles is from zero to 15. European needles are sized by their diameter in metric millimeters. The sizes are somewhat equivalent between the two standards for measurement. (See Photo B) However, there is no guarantee that a size 8 American will be the same size as a metric size 5, as the sizes often differ slightly from one manufacturer to another. The patterns in this book list the American size with the metric size following in parentheses.

Often, the size of the needle is not imprinted on the needle itself. You may want to invest in a needle sizer to help you determine the size of an unmarked needle if it gets separated from its packaging. (See Needle Sizer on page 15)

Needle Lengths

Just as knitting needles are available in more than one size or diameter, they are also available in more than one length. Straight needles come in lengths from 10" to 16". Circular needles are available in standard lengths of 16", 24", 29", and 36". Double-pointed needles can be found in 5", 7", and 10" lengths.

When you are considering the length of needle to use for your project, consider first the size of your project. It is better to select a needle length that is slightly shorter than the width of the project than to use one that is too long and ends up stretching the knitting. This applies especially when working with circular needles.

Needle Materials

Knitting needles are available in a variety of materials. Aluminum and plastic needles are common at craft stores and are the least expensive. For the avid knitter who may wish to invest a bit more money in her supplies, needles made of bamboo, exotic woods, and hand-blown glass are also available. Although an aluminum needle will knit a stitch the same as a bamboo needle, the feel of the tool, while being used, is the main difference.

Photo B

Knitting Needle Equivalency Chart

American	Metric
0	2mm
1	2.25mm
2	2.5mm
3	3mm
4	3.5mm
5	3.75mm
6	4mm
7	4.5mm
8	5mm
9	5.5mm
10	6mm
10½	6.5mm
10¾	7mm
11	8mm
13	9mm
15	10mm

Other Equipment

Blocking Pins

These pins, made specifically for knitting, are longer than dressmaker's pins and have large heads that will not get lost in the weave of the knitted fabric. They are used for pinning a piece in place for blocking and for pinning pieces together for sewing.

Cable Needles

These elongated crooked or "u"-shaped double-pointed needles are used for holding stitches while you are working a cable pattern.

Crochet Hook

A crochet hook is used for some finishing work and for recovering dropped stitches. For most projects, a medium-sized crochet hook will work best.

Knitting Bags

Because you will often be moving your knitting from place to place, you need a way to organize and carry all of your "stuff." Look for a bag that is large enough to hold your project, pattern, materials, and equipment. A bag with various-sized pockets is nice to have. Canvas or fabric totes work well as do backpacks designed for carrying school books.

You should also have a small zippered bag for carrying smaller items so they do not get lost at the bottom of your knitting bag.

Line Marker or Long Self-stick Notes

When working with charted patterns, it is helpful to have either a line marker or self-stick notes to keep track of your place on the chart.

Needle Sizer

Also called a "needle gauge," this tool with graduated holes will help you find the size of any unmarked knitting needles and help you determine if one needle marked size 6 is bigger than another needle also marked size 6. You should purchase a needle sizer marked for both American- and metric-sized needles.

Row Counters

Use row counters and markers to help you keep track of how many rows you have completed. Place a counter in the first stitch from where you want to count. Continue knitting and periodically stop, count 20 rows, and place another counter. In placing a counter every 20 rows, you will be able to count rows without having to start at the beginning each time.

Ruler or Tape Measure

You will need a small ruler or a tape measure marked in inches and centimeters for measuring gauge and checking project length.

Safety Pins

In knitting, safety pins are used in a number of different ways. They are often used as row counters and stitch markers. In patterns where just a few stitches need to be set aside, safety pins are ideal stitch holders. They are also handy for securing dropped stitches and pinning seams.

Scissors

The scissors you choose should be sharp. They are for cutting the yarn as you work. We recommend that you look for small portable scissors that will fit in your knitting bag. Some scissors are collapsible and others come with their own case to keep the tips from being exposed.

Stitch Holders

These extra-long safety pins are used for holding stitches that will be worked or finished off later. Stitch holders are available in lengths from 1¾" to 8".

Stitch Markers

A stitch marker is a small ring that you slip onto your knitting needle to help you keep track of stitches or places in your work that demand special attention such as the beginning and end of a repeat. When you come to a stitch marker, you slip it from the left-hand needle onto the right-hand needle and continue knitting. Stitch markers are available in different sizes and colors.

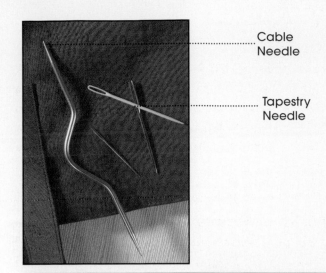

Cable Needle

Tapestry Needle

Tapestry Needle

A tapestry needle is used for weaving in yarn ends, sewing knitted pieces together, and embroidery work. This type of needle has a large eye that accommodates the yarn and a blunt point that helps you avoid splitting the yarn on the pieces you are sewing.

Yarn Bobbins

Yarn bobbins are small flat pieces of plastic on which you can wind a small amount of yarn. They are used when you are adding small areas of color in a pattern. Yarn bobbins are available in large and small sizes.

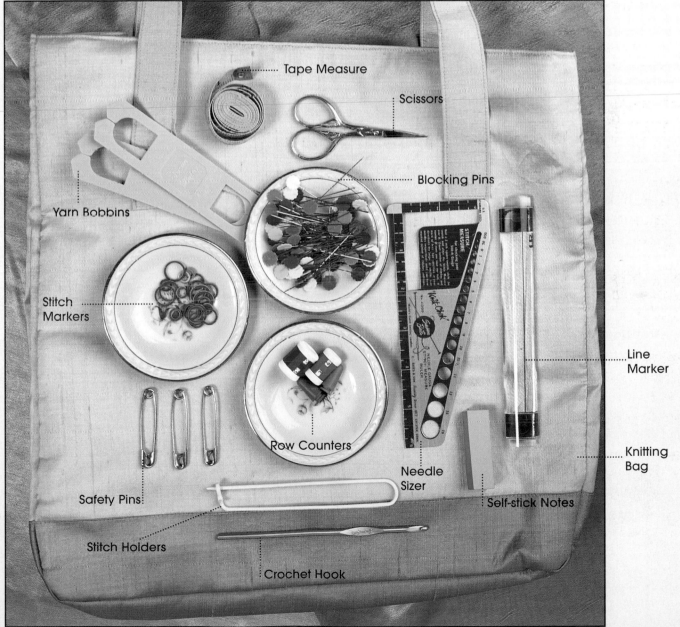

Tape Measure

Scissors

Blocking Pins

Yarn Bobbins

Stitch Markers

Line Marker

Row Counters

Needle Sizer

Knitting Bag

Safety Pins

Self-stick Notes

Stitch Holders

Crochet Hook

What do I need to know about yarn?

When selecting yarn for your project, there are a number of things to consider. There are many different gauges, colors, weights, thicknesses, fibers, combinations of fibers, and textures of yarn available for any knitting project.

Think about what you desire in the appearance of the piece you will be knitting. If you want to highlight the pattern of the knitting—cables, for example—a smooth-plied yarn in a solid color is the best choice. If you are more interested in showing off the color or texture of the yarn itself, knit in a simple pattern such as the stockinette stitch, and let the yarn do the shining. If you are doing work in which two colors are combined such as the intarsia pattern worked for the Stars & Stripes Baby Sweater on page 59, you should select a simple solid-colored yarn so your pattern will read well in the finished piece.

Often, a yarn will create varied and surprising effects when you knit it using different techniques. For example, when knitted in the round, variegated yarns will create a striped effect. Do not be afraid to experiment when you are unsure of how a yarn and a pattern will behave together. This is the sure way to determine if the combination will work or not. As an additional help, most knitting stores will have gauge samples or samples of the yarns made into projects available for you to study.

The patterns in this book will provide the necessary information for selecting the exact yarn to create a project like the sample shown. However, you may use the following information to make some choices of your own and thereby create a project that is one of a kind.

Yarn Packaging

Yarn is sold in a ball, a hank, or a skein. (See Photo C) It is measured for a project by weight. The weight per unit varies with each manufacturer. The patterns in this book list the required number of yarn units along with the weight of the yarn.

Photo C — Hank — Skein — Ball

Gauge

To correctly size your project, you need to know the gauge or tension of the yarn. Gauge indicates the number of stitches and rows per inch and is determined by the size of the needles and weight of the yarn. However, all yarns with the same gauge are not necessarily created equal. When deciding between two yarns that have the same gauge, one yarn may be a better choice than the other. The simple fact that two yarns have the same gauge does not necessarily mean that they will yield the same look, texture, or drape to the finished piece.

Yarn Weights

Yarn weight refers to the thickness of the strand of yarn. This thickness largely determines its gauge or how many stitches it will take to make up an inch of knitting.

For example, a medium-weight yarn may have a gauge of five stitches and seven rows to the inch, resulting in 35 stitches to the square inch. However, a heavy- or bulky-weight yarn, when worked on the same size needles, may only work up three stitches and five rows to the inch, resulting in 15 stitches to the square inch. Thus, it will take less knitting with the bulky yarn than with the medium-weight yarn to stitch the same number of inches.

While there are no standardized categories for yarn weights, there are generalized terms that describe yarns by thickness and size of needle they are usually worked on. (See Fig. 4) The label on the yarn will have this information.

Fig. 4		
Yarn	Needles	Stitches per Inch
Baby/fingering	1–3	7–8
Sport/baby	3–6	5–6
Chunky	5–7	5–5½
Worsted	7–9	4–5
Bulky	10–11	3–3½

Yarn is also made up of plies. The number of plies is the number of strands of yarn twisted together.

Tightly twisted and multi-plied yarns are generally strong, smooth, and even. A loosely twisted or single-ply yarn will have more loft, softness, and warmth than the tighter-twisted yarn, but the strand will be easier to split with needles.

Although the number of plies is relative to the strength of the yarn, it does not necessarily imply thickness. A yarn with four plies of thin strands can be thinner than a heavier-weight single-ply yarn.

Yarn Fibers

Yarn is made both from natural fibers such as wool and cotton, and from synthetic fibers that are processed from petroleum, coal, or wood. The type of fiber or fibers used to make up the yarn is also referred to as its "content." It is the yarn's content that determines the look, feel, and wearable comfort of the finished piece. (See Photo D)

Photo D — Wool, Synthetic Acrylic, Cotton

Natural Fibers

Wool is made from the fleece of sheep. It remains the most popular fiber for use in knitting. It is a good insulator because it traps air into pockets created by microfibers, making it cool in summer and warm in winter. It returns to its original shape after being stretched or bent because the fibers do not break. A little steam will smooth out uneven stitches. Wool is soft to the touch and comes in a wide variety of colors and weights.

Cotton is a plant fiber. Plant fibers are smooth and slippery. A natural sheen and fondness for dyes make cotton popular for knitting.

Rayon is fabricated from the cellulose of plants and not spun by the plant itself. It is very slick and has a beautiful luster.

Silk is not a plant fiber, but tends to have many of the same traits. It has a luster that is beautiful to look at and luxurious to wear.

Other natural fibers such as alpaca, angora, camel, cashmere, lamb's wool, and mohair all possess desirable qualities in softness, weight, and durability. The cost of these fibers is considerably higher, but the quality of the piece may merit the extra cost.

Synthetic Fibers

Synthetics are man-made fibers—polyester, acrylic, and nylon. They can be made to mimic the look and feel of natural fibers. Synthetic yarns are less likely to cause allergies. However, synthetics "pill" more easily, and if heated, lose all resilience and become flat and cannot be revived.

Blended Fibers

The combination of two or more of these fibers is called a "blend." Cotton is often blended with other natural fibers to counteract its tendency to stretch out over time and not bounce back. Silk also is often blended with other natural fibers to counteract some of its less desirable traits such as its slipperiness and tendency to unravel quickly if a stitch is dropped.

Yarn Textures

Yarn textures are directly related to their weight and fiber content. However, it is the technique used in the spinning process that creates individual textures.

Brushed yarns and hairy yarns such as mohair and angora, are made from natural fibers. Mohair yarns are made from the wool of young angora goats. Mohair yarn is a fuzzy, lightweight yarn that dyes easily and is available in almost every color. They are high-volume yarns that yield a soft, furry look.

Bouclé yarns, which include bouclé, gimp, and loop varieties, are generally made from wool or wool blends. Bouclé is referred to as a specialty yarn as it is made to have irregular loops that are twisted around a thinner "support thread." The construction of this yarn gives it a bumpy appearance.

Chenille yarns have a plush, velvet-like surface and are made from cotton, rayon, or acrylic. They are very soft and slick and can be a bit difficult to work with for a first-time knitting experience.

Felted yarns are treated in the strand to look like a felted piece of knitting. They are soft and slightly fuzzy.

Heather yarns are yarns spun with a mix of dyed or naturally gray fleece. This process gives the yarn a muted watercolor-like appearance.

Linen yarns are very smooth, somewhat shiny and relatively stiff. Linen yarn is spun from flax which breathes well, making linen garments cool and comfortable to wear.

Mélange yarns are made up of a mixture of different-colored fibers. The fibers are combed together and then spun into a yarn.

Mouliné yarns are made up of two or more different colors or filaments that are twisted together. A mouliné yarn that is made up of different fibers is quite interesting when it is dyed, as each fiber takes on the dye in a different way.

Nubby yarns are spun with irregular, wick-like sections that are usually dyed a different color.

Ribbon yarns are commonly made from cotton or rayon. They can be knit or woven and are available in different widths.

Tweed yarns are a category of nubby yarns. Usually made of wool, the main strand in a tweed is of one color while the flecks or nubs are of another color.

Variegated or ombré yarns are dyed in several different colors or shades of the same color, which appear at regular or irregular intervals.

Wick yarns are soft, open, and loosely spun. They have thick nubs and are available in solid and multicolored varieties. They yield a very primitive and rustic look.

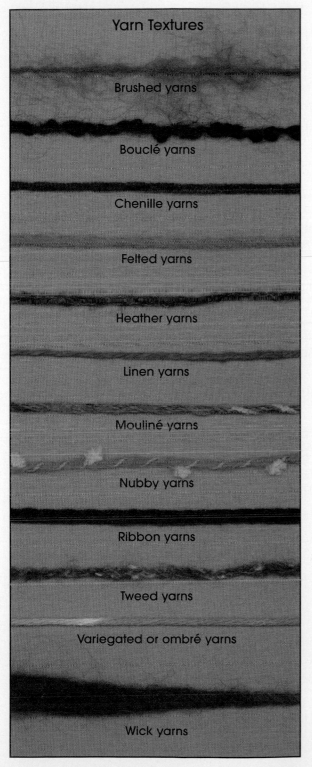

Yarn Textures

Brushed yarns

Bouclé yarns

Chenille yarns

Felted yarns

Heather yarns

Linen yarns

Mouliné yarns

Nubby yarns

Ribbon yarns

Tweed yarns

Variegated or ombré yarns

Wick yarns

Yarn Colors

Choosing colors that will go together in a knitted fabric can be overwhelming when you are standing in a yarn shop surrounded by baskets and bins overflowing with all colors of yarn. Oftentimes yarns that seem agreeable together in the shop take on an entirely different personality when they are lying side by side as neighboring stitches in a particular pattern.

Successful use of color in knitting comes with practice, through trial and error, and by serendipity (happy accidents). There really is no right or wrong, only what pleases you and what does not. The ability to choose and combine colors on your own comes with experience and diligence—keep trying! Begin with how you feel about a color or combination of colors, add a bit of basic information about how colors work together, and you have the foundation for selecting the perfect yarn for your project from the millions of colors available.

A color wheel can be a big help to you when trying to choose colors that go together. Remember that all colors come from the three primary colors: blue, red, and yellow. Hue is the name of a color. Value is the degree of lightness or darkness of a color, and intensity is the brightness or dullness of a hue. Complementary colors are the colors that are directly across the color wheel from each other. Analogous colors are those situated next to each other. You can see this visually with the use of a standard 12-color color wheel. (See Fig. 5)

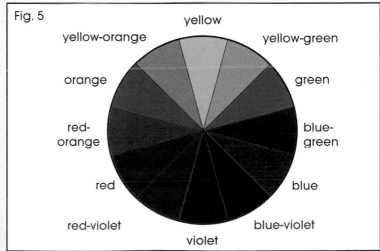

Fig. 5

yellow

yellow-orange

yellow-green

orange

green

red-orange

blue-green

red

blue

red-violet

blue-violet

violet

You may want to try using analogous colors together. Be aware that when you combine these colors from any point on the color wheel, you are selecting colors that share the same base color. Subsequently, the color combination will express itself in a subtle manner and often reflect a mood or temperature. For example, a sweater that is knit in shades of blue will communicate a cool, mellow, or melancholy feeling, while one in shades of red will present itself as warm, more lively, and upbeat.

If you use complementary colors together in a piece, the resulting combination will convey a feeling of boldness and strength. Complementary colors, because they are of the same value and intensity, balance each other. They keep your eye moving from one color to the next and back again.

Consider also the degree of contrast in your color combinations. Contrast is what gives a combination interest. Contrast can come from combining two different complementary hues such as blue and orange (high contrast), or from combining two values of the same hue such as red and pink (low contrast).

Take time to experiment with a variety of colors. When you knit a color combination that is pleasing to you, see if you can determine what it is that made it work—the hue, the value, the intensity, or a combination of these.

Finally, when you come to the point of knitting a project, use a bit of caution. It is a good idea to make a sample first, using the yarn you have chosen. This way you avoid knitting an entire piece only to find you dislike the color combination.

How do I prepare my yarn for knitting?

You need to look at the yarn you purchased and decide whether it is a ball, a hank, or a skein.

Ball of Yarn

Yarn wound in a ball can be pulled from the center or unrolled from the outside.

Hank of Yarn

Yarn in a hank is wound in a large circle that is then twisted and knotted together at the ends. This makes pulling yarn directly from the hank nearly impossible. Before beginning to knit, unfold the hank of yarn into a large circle. Have a friend hold the circle on both hands, then wind the yarn into a ball. (See Fig. 6)

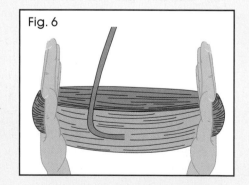

Fig. 6

Skein of Yarn

If the yarn is in a skein, you can simply pull the end of the yarn from the center and start knitting.

How do I hold the yarn while I am knitting?

There are two methods for holding the yarn during the process of knitting. The first is the English method and the second is the Continental method.

Note: The bulk of the drawn diagrams shown in this book depict the English method of holding the yarn.

English Method

After casting on the number of stitches indicated, you will hold the needle with the stitches in your left hand the empty needle in your right hand.

a. You will begin knitting by inserting the right-hand needle into the first stitch on the left-hand needle from front to back. (See Fig. 7)

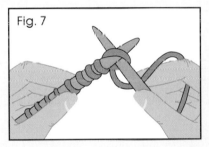

Fig. 7

b. Then, with your right index finger, you will wrap the yarn around the right-hand needle tip from back to front, over the needle, and to the right again. (See Fig. 8)

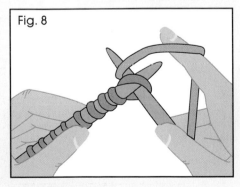

Fig. 8

c. Keeping slight tension on the yarn, you will bring the tip of the right-hand needle with its wrap of yarn through the loop on the left-hand needle to the front, and slide the right-hand needle to the right until the old loop on the left-hand needle drops off. (See Fig. 9) You will continue in this manner (needle in, wrap yarn around, new loop through, old loop off) until all the stitches from the left-hand needle have been knitted and moved onto the right-hand needle. Turn the work so the needle with all the stitches is in your left hand again, keeping the yarn toward the back and in your right hand.

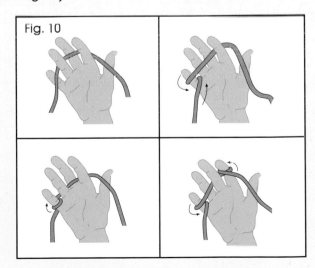

Fig. 9

d. To keep adequate tension on the yarn when using the English method, try weaving it through the fingers of your right hand, using one of the methods shown. (See Fig. 10)

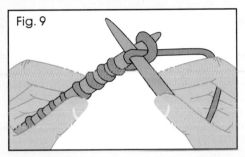

Fig. 10

Continental Method

a. To knit using the Continental method, you will hold the yarn in your left hand behind the needle with the cast-on stitches. Wind the yarn around your left pinky finger and over your left index finger. (See Fig. 11)

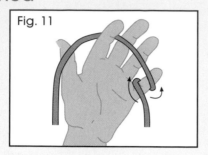

Fig. 11

b. As for the English method, you will begin knitting by inserting the right-hand needle into the first stitch on the left-hand needle from front to back. (See Fig. 12) Then, you will simply rotate the tip of the right-hand needle to the right and under the yarn waiting on your left index finger, creating a wrap of yarn around the right-hand needle.

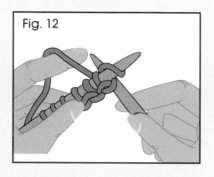

Fig. 12

c. You will bring the tip of the right-hand needle with its wrap of yarn through the loop on the left-hand needle to the front, and slide the right-hand needle to the right until the old loop on the left-hand needle drops off. (See Fig. 13) You will continue in this manner (in, around, new loop through, old loop off) until all the stitches from the left-hand needle have been knitted and moved onto the right-hand needle. Turn the work so the needle with all the stitches is in your left hand again.

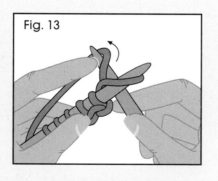

Fig. 13

How do I select and read a stitch pattern?

Selecting a Pattern

Pattern selection is usually determined by the skill level and personal preferences of the knitter. Most patterns available in knit shops are marked, "beginner," "intermediate," or "advanced." Beginner patterns are typically worked with basic stitches and have minimal shaping and simple finishing. Intermediate patterns involve more-complicated stitches, but have fairly simple shaping and finishing. Patterns marked advanced are challenging projects that have complicated stitches and require detailed shaping and finishing.

Whether you are right-handed or left-handed, knitting is a craft that requires the use of both hands. Generally, knitting patterns are written for the right-handed knitter (working stitches from the left-hand needle to the right-hand needle). If you are left-handed, the working of the stitches may seem awkward at first. However, as you become more accustomed to the method and rhythm of knitting, you will soon develop a series of movements that feel comfortable and natural to you.

Stitch Patterns

A stitch pattern is a method for describing how to accomplish a desired texture or pattern in your knitted fabric. Stitch patterns are based on repeats—*stitch repeats* and *row repeats*. A given stitch sequence repeats *horizontally* across a row. A series of rows of given stitch sequences repeats *vertically*. Stitch pattern instructions show you the stitches and rows that make up a single repeat. Subsequently, you are then given instructions for the number of times the repeat should be worked to complete the pattern.

A stitch pattern will begin by giving the total number of stitches that should be put or "cast" on the knitting needle for working the first row. This number is figured by knowing the number of stitches in a single repeat, multiplying that by the number of repeats, and adding any additional stitches required to complete that row in the pattern. For example, 31 stitches on the first row is equal to a sequence of 10 stitches that repeats three times and requires one additional stitch to complete the row ((10 x 3) +1).

Patterns are available in two basic formats—the written pattern and the charted pattern. Some knitters prefer written instructions while others like to follow a charted "picture" of the pattern. Up until the last few decades, stitch patterns that are now referred to as "vintage" were completely written out. Although stitch patterns are still largely written out, a pattern that is complex and requires a lot of detailed instruction is likely to be charted out. You should be familiar with both ways of describing a pattern. Then you can convert a chart into written instructions and vice versa if you wish to do so.

Reading Written Patterns

The written pattern consists of instructions written out to follow the progression of the work, row by row, for a single repeat. They are usually divided into sections such as left and right, front and back, and sleeves. Standardized abbreviations of terms and phrases are used to help condense the length of the instructions. (See Abbreviated Terms & Phrases on page 26)

The key to understanding written instructions is paying attention to commas and asterisks. The text that is written between commas is a single step. An asterisk (*) indicates that whatever follows gets repeated (rep)—usually the "*" indicates that what follows is the stitch repeat.

The following example shows a stitch pattern in written form:

Row 1 (RS): *K3, p3, rep from * to end of row.
Row 2 (WS): *P3, k3, rep from * to end of row.

In plain English, this pattern directs you to work the first row (with the right side facing you) and knit three stitches, then purl three stitches, then repeat the stitches from the asterisk again to the end of the row. (Your row would have to be a multiple of six stitches for these instructions to come out evenly.) On the next row (wrong side facing now), you begin by purling three stitches, then knitting three stitches, then repeating the stitches from the asterisk again to the end of the row.

Reading Charted Patterns

Patterns that create a specific knitted pattern such as a cable or that call for frequent color changes are often better represented and easier to read when they are charted on a grid.

A chart is made up of individual squares on a grid. Each square represents a stitch. Symbols and colors placed within the squares are used to indicate how to work the stitch. Although the symbols may vary from chart to chart, each pattern will provide a key that explains the symbol or color found on the chart. Each horizontal line on the charted pattern represents a row of knitting.

Find the key to the chart first. Then, if the first row is a right-side row, start at the *bottom* right-hand corner of the chart and read to the *left*. Read the second row from left to right. (If the first row is a wrong-side row, the first row of the chart reads from left to right.)

Charts, like written patterns, are based on repeats. If the design uses a repeating pattern, the chart will usually show a single or double repeat and not the entire piece.

It is important to remember that charts represent the pattern as viewed on the right side of the knitted fabric. This means that *on wrong side rows* (from left to right) you must *purl any stitch that has a knit symbol and knit any stitch that has a purl symbol*. At first, this may seem a bit confusing, but as you continue working with the chart, you will soon become accustomed to the method. The pattern key will help you remember.

If you are knitting in the round, you can follow the chart without worrying about whether you have the wrong side or right side of the fabric facing you. (See Moose Christmas Stocking on page 72 for knitting in the round).

This chart shows the same pattern as in the previous section on following written patterns, but it presents this pattern in charted form:

| | | ★ | ★ | ★ | | | ★ | ★ | ★ | 2 |
| | | ★ | ★ | ★ | | | ★ | ★ | ★ | 1 |

☐ Knit on RS
Purl on WS

★ Purl on RS
Knit on WS

Combination Stitch Patterns

Often a pattern will be a combination of the two formats with some of the instructions written out and some of them charted. The pattern may include a chart to show a particular stitch, a cable, or a color pattern. It may also represent an unusual feature of a garment.

Note: Purchase either a line marker or long self-stick notes to help keep track of your place on the chart. Position the marker or note along the row directly above the row that you are currently working. This way you can see where you are in the pattern by comparing the rows you have already worked in your piece to the rows you currently see on the chart.

Pattern Contents

Generally, all sizes and numbers given in the pattern instructions are for the smallest size. Larger sizes, if applicable, are listed in order in parentheses. If only one number is given, it applies to all sizes.

Note: Before you begin knitting, it is a good idea to highlight or circle the size you will be making throughout the pattern to eliminate errors. (See Fig. 14-A)

Your pattern will tell you what size needles are recommended. (See Fig. 14-B) It will also tell you how many stitches to cast on and instruct you, row by row, what stitches to use, or it will simply give you one stitch and tell you to knit for a determined number of inches. (See Fig. 14-C)

The pattern will also tell you when to start forming elements of the project such as armholes, and give you the order for knitting separate pieces of a garment, i.e. the sleeves first, then the body. (See Fig. 14-D)

Gauge Notation

Your pattern will include a gauge notation (the number of stitches and rows per inch) for the weight of yarn and size of needles required to make the sample. (See Fig. 14-E) You may use the gauge provided as a guide, but the most reliable thing to do is to knit your own "gauge swatch" with the yarn you have chosen before starting any project. This way you can see if your tension equals the gauge called for in the pattern.

We recommend that you knit a square in the pattern or stitches indicated that is five to 10 stitches and five to 10 rows larger than that called for in the pattern's gauge notation. Press the finished square under a damp cloth and allow it to dry. Mark out the stitches indicated for gauge with blocking pins and measure the inches with your ruler or tape measure. (See Fig. 15)

Fig. 14

2
technique

How do I increase stitches and cable cast on?

What you need to get started:

Knitting needles:
Size 8 (5mm)
Yarn:
100% cotton, 84 yds (77m),
50 gm; blue grey (MC),
6 balls; chicory (CC),
1 ball

B

To make a shape beyond a square, you can either increase or decrease the number of stitches that were orignally cast onto your needle. For this cardigan with raglan sleeves, two methods are used to add onto the original number of stitches—increasing one stitch at a time and casting on an additional number of stitches at the end of a knitted row.

Toddler Cardigan

Designed by Song Palmese

Skill level: beginner

Finished measurements: Child's size 2T, chest: 11", length: 13". Only one size is given; all numbers given refer to the one size. If necessary, adjust needle size to obtain the correct gauge. ·········· A

Here's how:

Finding the Gauge ·········· E
1. Refer to Gauge Notation on page 25. Refer to Technique 1, Cast On, Knit, and Garter Stitch on pages 41–42. Using 18 st = 4" with size 8 needles, CO and work in garter stitch to create a gauge swatch.

Knitting the Cardigan Back ·········· D
2. CO 51 sts with MC. Beg at the waist, work in garter stitch until piece measures 6" (42 rows or 21 ridges).

44

C

Fig. 15

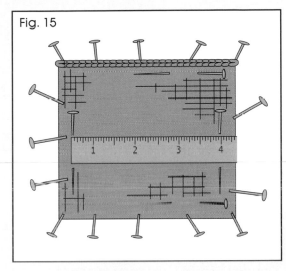

If you have too many stitches per inch, you are working too tightly. You need to stitch with less tension or switch to larger needles. Similarly, if you have too few stitches per inch, you are working too loosely. In this case, you need to stitch with greater tension or switch to smaller needles. Some of the most experienced knitters attribute the success of their pieces to creating a gauge swatch before beginning so as to accurately gauge the size and tension of the stitches.

Abbreviated Terms & Phrases

The terms and phrases included in the following list are commonly abbreviated in knitting patterns. You may wish to photocopy this list to have on hand while knitting the projects until you become accustomed to working with the abbreviations.

beg	begin(ning)
BO	bind off
Cable CO	cable cast on
CC	coordinating color
cm	centimeter(s)
CO	cast on
cont	continu(e)(ing)
dec	decreas(e)(ing)
gm	gram(s)
inc	increas(e)(ing)
k	knit
k2tog	knit two stitches together
m	meter(s)
M1	make one
MC	main color
mm	millimeter(s)
oz	ounce(s)
p	purl
p2tog	purl two stitches together
patt	pattern
psso	pass slipped stitch(es) over
rem	remaining stitches
rep	repeat
RS	right side
sl	slip
ssk	slip, slip, knit
st(s)	stitch(es)
WS	wrong side
yd(s)	yard(s)
yo	yarn over
*	repeat directions following * as indicated
[ ]	repeat directions inside brackets as many times as indicated

as established once the pattern has set up a series of steps or patterns to work, it will tell you to continue working *as established*, rather than repeating the information row by row

at same time indicates that two things should be happening at the same time. For example, you may be instructed to work a series of stitches that make up a pattern while, at the same time, you are to begin increasing the number of stitches on each row.

break disconnect yarn that is being worked from the skein either by breaking it or cutting it

change to indicates a change in needle size. Simply place needle holding the work in your left hand and begin working into the stitches as instructed with the new-sized needle in your right hand. Do not slide work off old size and onto new size.

knitwise insert right-hand needle as if to knit (from front to back and left to right)

purlwise insert right-hand needle as if to purl (from back to front and right to left)

reverse shaping commonly used to as a way to condense instructions for pieces that mirror each other—to avoid writing the shaping pattern out again only in reverse order, the instructions direct you to figure it out on your own. Simply study the indicated set of instructions and work the piece row by row, but from the last stitch to the first stitch (reverse order).

work as for work in the same manner and stitches as for the indicated previously worked piece

work even(ly) continue in the specified pattern without increasing or decreasing (using same number of stitches)

How do I start a new skein of yarn?

Starting/Joining a New Skein of Yarn

If you find you are running out of one skein of yarn and need to start a fresh one, there are a couple of ways to do this.

The first and preferred method is to end with the old skein at the end of a WS row. Do not worry about using up all the yarn on this skein. It is better to waste a bit of yarn than to arrive at its end in the middle of a row or on the right side of the pattern. Leave a long enough tail to work with, but not so long that it will be mistaken for the working yarn. Start the new skein at the beginning of the next row and again leave a tail. (See Fig. 16) Tie the two tails into a square knot (right over left, left over right) and leave the ends for weaving into the knitting later.

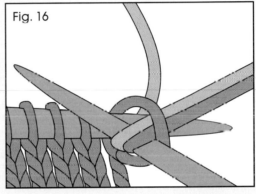

Fig. 16

The second method is to leave a tail from the yarn in the first skein wherever its end may fall, pick up the second skein and, leaving a tail from it also, knit the next couple of stitches. (See Fig. 17) Go back and tie the two ends in a square knot and weave the ends in later. Try to keep the knot and the ends on the WS of the work.

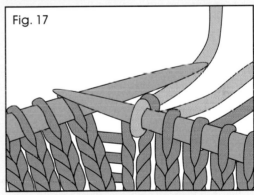

Fig. 17

If you come to a break in the yarn in the skein that was tied in a knot by the manufacturer, do not just knit it into the work as that knot will probably not hold. Untie or cut the knot out and retie it using a square knot. Weave the ends into the piece later.

How do I fix mistakes?

Troubleshooting

Although knitting is relatively easy, mistakes are inevitable and repairs may need to be made in the course of completing a project.

For example, in moving your project from place to place between knitting sessions, it is possible for the needle to slip out of the stitches. Or, during knitting, a stitch can be accidentally dropped off the needle, leaving a hole in the cloth that will eventually cause the piece to unravel. Or, you may make a mistake and not discover it until long after it is made, requiring that you take out several rows to fix it.

As you begin knitting it may be helpful to check your work by counting the stitches after each row. One stitch more or less than you cast on means that something is wrong in the last row worked. After a while, counting stitches will not be necessary. Your fingers will alert you to a missed move, and you will be catching mistakes before you have proceeded too far into your project.

If you count the number of stitches on the knitting needle and discover that you have one stitch less than you should have, you have probably dropped a stitch. Carefully spread out the stitches along the needle and slowly scan the row(s) below the needle until the dropped stitch is located. Carefully work the tip of a safety pin into the dropped stitch, securing and stretching it out. Refer to the correct method for retrieving the dropped stitch.

Correcting a Dropped Stitch

The method used to correct a dropped stitch depends on whether you want to knit the stitch or purl it. *The unworked horizontal strand of yarn will* *either be behind or in front of the dropped stitch. If there is no sign of an unknitted strand, place the stitch back on the left-hand needle.*

Knitting a dropped stitch

If the purl side is facing you or you are working in the garter stitch, correct the dropped stitch as follows:

a.   Insert right-hand needle tip into front of dropped (pinned) stitch.

Note: If you look behind the stitch you will notice, a horizontal strand of yarn that did not get wrapped and pulled through as a new stitch.

b.   Move the right-hand needle tip under this unworked strand from the front, placing the strand and the stitch on the needle. (See Fig. 18)

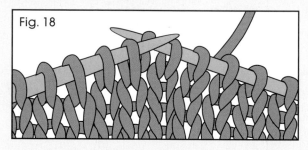

Fig. 18

c.   Insert the left-hand needle into the stitch from the back and pull it over the strand. (See Fig. 19)

Note: The strand has become a stitch.

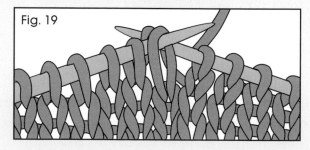

Fig. 19

d.   Place the new stitch on the left-hand needle. Make certain that you have made a smooth V stitch. Continue working pattern as indicated.

Purling a dropped stitch

If the purl side is facing or you are working in stockinette stitch, correct the dropped stitch as follows:

a. Insert the right-hand needle tip into the dropped stitch and the unworked strand from the back.

Note: If you look in front of the stitch you will notice a horizontal strand of yarn that did not get wrapped and pulled through as a new stitch.

b. Using the left-hand needle, pull the dropped stitch over the strand and off the needle, forming a new stitch on the right-hand needle. (See Fig. 20)

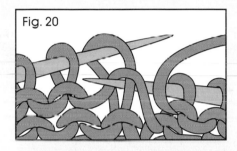
Fig. 20

c. Place the new stitch on the left-hand needle. (See Fig. 21) Continue working pattern as indicated.

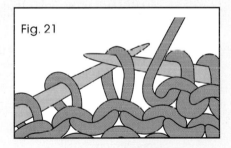
Fig. 21

Correcting a Dropped Stitch in a Row Below

If you notice a dropped stitch in the row below, continue working until you reach the pinned stitch.

Correcting a Dropped Stitch from Several Rows Below

If the dropped stitch has worked itself down several rows, find the dropped stitch and secure it with a safety pin. Work to the stitch count where the stitch dropped. The wayward stitch will be at the bottom of a "ladder" of unworked strands. Each strand represents a row. (See Fig. 22)

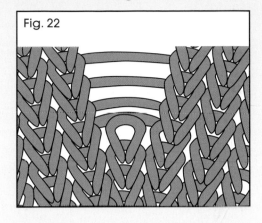
Fig. 22

Correcting a dropped stitch in stockinette stitch

Correct a dropped stitch from the knit side using the following method:

a. Using a crochet hook, come up through the pinned stitch and pick up the bottom strand in the ladder. (See Fig. 23)

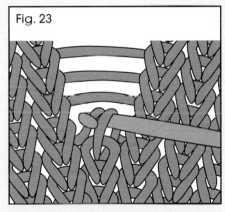
Fig. 23

b. Pull the strand through the stitch, forming a new stitch. Continue to pull each strand in the ladder through the loop on the crochet hook until the last strand has been worked.

c. Pull on the work in each direction after correcting a dropped stitch to blend the stitches.

d. Slip the last loop on the crochet hook back onto the left-hand knitting needle. Continue working pattern as indicated.

Correcting a dropped stitch in garter stitch

Correct a dropped stitch from the purl side using the following method:

a. Alternate the direction from which the ladder strands are pulled through the dropped stitch. Pull strand through the front of the stitch for a knit stitch. Pull strand through the back of the stitch for a purl stitch.

b. Determine whether to pull the first strand at the bottom ladder through the secured stitch from the front or the back. To do this, follow the bottom strand to the side to see what the stitch connected to it looks like. If necessary, pull gently on the strand to locate the neighboring stitches. (See Fig. 24)

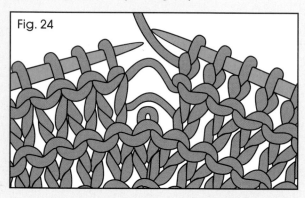

Fig. 24

Note: If the base of the next stitch is the bottom of a "V," it is a knit stitch and the dropped stitch should be picked up from the front. If the base stitch is a bump, insert the crochet hook into the stitch from back to front (toward you), pick up the strand, and pull it through. (See Fig. 25) Make certain the rescued stitch matches the ones next to it or follows the established pattern.

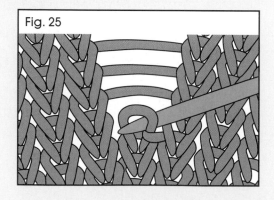

Fig. 25

c. Alternate pulling stitches from each direction until the last strand has been pulled through. Put the last loop onto the left-hand knitting needle. Continue working as indicated.

Correcting Too Many Stitches

If too many stitches are on the needle, the yarn may have crossed the needle while you were not paying a attention, inadvertently increasing the number of stitches or it could mean that the wrap of yarn has not quite made it through the old stitch. The stitch will need to be ripped out.

Ripping out: stitch by stitch

If the mistake is on the row you are working on, rip back one stitch at a time, using the following method:

a. With the knit or purl side facing, insert the left-hand needle tip from front to back into the stitch below the one on the right-hand needle. (See Fig. 26 and Fig. 27)

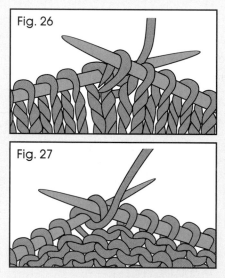

Fig. 26

Fig. 27

b. Slide the right-hand needle out of the stitch and gently rip, or pull the working yarn to undo the stitch.

c. Continue to rip back, stitch by stitch, to the point of the mistake. Continue working pattern as indicated.

Ripping out: row by row

If the mistake is located several rows below the one you are working, rip out the necessary rows, using the following method:

a.   Locate the row with the mistake. Mark the mistake with a safety pin.

b.   Slide the knitting needle out of the stitches. Gently rip, or pull the working yarn to undo the stitches, until you are on the row above the mistake. Rip to the end of the row.

Note: Gathering the work loosely in your left hand while gently pulling the yarn away will keep the work from stretching and pulling other stitches out.

c.   Hold your knitting with the working yarn on the right (flip it over if it is on the left). Insert the tip of the needle into the first stitch on the row below (from back to front toward you).

d.   Pull on the yarn to unravel the stitch. (See Fig. 28) Make certain to have one stitch on the right-hand needle. Continue to rip back, stitch by stitch, to the point of the mistake. Rip out the mistake. Continue working pattern as indicated.

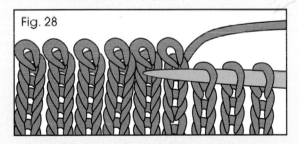

Fig. 28

Tips for correcting too many stitches

• Pick up the strands of yarn in the proper order. Pulling a loop through from a strand in the wrong row will cause more problems.

• Do not let the needle penetrate the yarn being used. Some yarn, especially plied ones, are prone to splitting.

• Make certain to go in and out of the holes in the stitches, leaving the yarn strand intact. Avoid piercing the yarn with the knitting needle.

• Use a needle several sizes smaller to pick up the last row of the ripped-out knitting. Change to the regular-sized needle when working the next row.

• Practice ripping out a little of your work on a practice piece before starting a project.

How do I finish my knitted pieces?

Weaving in Yarn Ends & Tails

Upon completing a knitted piece, you will likely find that there are several yarn ends that need to be woven into the piece before you can begin sewing up seams or assembling pieces together.

Using a tapestry needle, weave in all ends and tails back through completed knitting about 3" deep and cut off excess. (See Fig. 29).

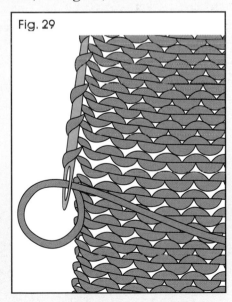

Fig. 29

Blocking

Blocking is the term used for smoothing out and flattening the knitted pieces so that they can be easily assembled or joined together. It streamlines the task of construction. If you are not inclined to do this yourself, most knit shops offer this service for a fee.

Blocking Equipment

Blocking board—a piece of Styrofoam® board insulation cut 36" x 54"

Blocking pins—to secure the project to the board

Clean damp white cloths or white towels

Craft knife and straightedge—to score 1" grid lines on surface of Styrofoam® board

Steam iron

Blocking Method

Using the craft knife and straightedge, score 1" grid lines horizontally and vertically on the surface of the Styrofoam® board.

Note: Do not use ink on the board as the ink could bleed onto the fabric.

Line the knitted project up with the grid lines and pin to the board as indicated by the finished measurements.

After the project has been pinned to size on the board, place damp cloths on the project and allow to dry overnight.

Hold an iron above the project—do not place the iron directly on knitting—and allow steam to penetrate the fabric. Move to the next section and repeat until finished. Allow to dry again before removing pins.

Note: Wool and cotton are typically the only fibers that take steaming well. If you use a steam iron, be certain to check the care label on the yarn before beginning.

Assembling/Sewing Seams

The following methods work with the structure of stitches, creating seams that are smooth, flexible and sometimes invisible. If possible, sew the pieces together with the same yarn used in the project. If the yarn is heavy or single ply, use a finer yarn in the same fiber in a similar color.

Order of sweater assembly

a. Tack down any pockets and work pocket trims or embroidery details on sweater pieces before seaming them together.

b. Join stitches head to head. (See Fig. 30)

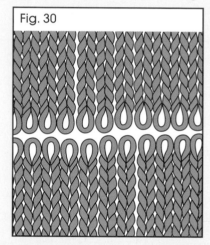
Fig. 30

c. Join stitches side to side. (See Fig. 31)

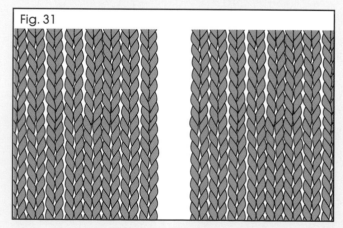
Fig. 31

d. Join stitches head to side. (See Fig. 32)

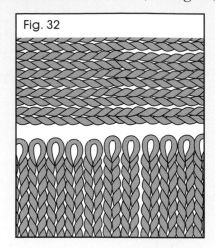

Fig. 32

e. Join backs to fronts at shoulder.

f. Attach sleeve to sweater body.

g. Sew side and sleeve seams.

h. Sew on buttons if desired.

Joining stitches head to head

Joining stitches head to head can be done with either the three-needle bind-off method or the grafting method.

The three-needle bind-off method for joining stitches head to head uses three needles, one for each shoulder—front and back and one for working the actual bind-off. This method creates a stable and visible seam.

The grafting method for joining stitches head to head uses a tapestry needle, which is blunt, to avoid piercing yarn. This method creates a stretchy seam that is almost invisible, especially when using heavier yarn. Grafting allows two complex patterns to be joined.

Three-needle bind-off method

Note: If you do not have three needles the same size, use a smaller one for holding the stitches of one or both of the pieces to be bound off. Use the regular-sized needle to bind off.

a. For each piece, thread open stitches of piece onto one needle. Thread first needle through open stitches on the first piece, having the tip come out where the tail is. Thread the second needle through the second piece. Make certain the needle tips will point in the same direction when pieces are arranged right sides together.

Note: If you left a long tail end on the piece, use it to work the bind-off. If you have not left a tail end for this maneuver, start working with a new yarn strand and weave in the end later.

b. Insert the third needle knitwise into the first stitch on both needles. (See Fig. 33)

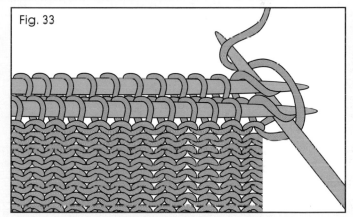

Fig. 33

c. Wrap yarn around the right-hand needle as if ready to knit, drawing the loop through both stitches. Knit and bind off as usual, but working one stitch from each left-hand needle at the same time.

d. Knit the next pair of stitches together in the same way.

e. Using tip of either left-hand needle, go into the first stitch knitted on right-hand needle. Lift it over the second stitch then off the needle.

f.   Continue to knit one from each of the left-hand needles and bind off one.

Grafting method
a.   Lay pieces on work surface with right sides up and stitches head to head, designating one top and one bottom.

b.   Thread the tapestry needle with working yarn.

Note: If you left a long tail end on the piece you will begin grafting from, use it. If not, start a new yarn strand and weave in the end later, grafting stitches from right to left.

c.   Starting in the bottom piece, insert the needle up through the first loop on the right. Pull the yarn through to leave a tail.

d.   Insert the needle up through the first loop on the right of the upper piece. Pull the yarn through.

e.   Insert the needle down into the first loop on the bottom piece (the same loop you began in) and come up through the loop next to it. Pull the yarn through.

f.   Insert the needle down into the first loop on the upper piece (the same one you came up from before) and up through the stitch next to it. Pull the yarn through. (See Fig. 34)

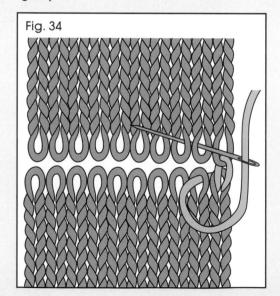

Fig. 34

g.   Repeat e–f.

h.   When you reach the last stitches, insert the needle down into the last stitch on the bottom piece then down into the last stitch on the upper piece. Weave the end in along the side loops. Trim end if necessary.

Although "real" grafting is done between two sets of free loops, a row of free loops can also be grafted to a selvage or bound-off edge. "Fake" grafting uses the same technique but with solid rows and edges, rather than free loops, on both sides.

Tips for Grafting:
• Check that the tips of needles are pointing to the right. Transfer to spare needles if necessary.

• Use yarn for grafting coming out of one of the two rows to be grafted. Four times the width of the rows is needed.

• Keep tension even and loose. Ease all the excess yarn towards the left edge with a cable needle or sewing needle. The grafted row should look the same as the rest.

• If one needle has more stitches than the other, work together two stitches of the longer row at regular intervals.

• Grafting at a change-of-pattern line will hide changes in fabric direction, making a different tension in the grafting row less noticeable.

Joining stitches side to side

Joining stitches side to side can be done with the mattress stitch, or figure eight. The mattress stitch makes an invisible and flexible seam.

Note: If you have left a tail of yarn at the cast-on edge, use it to get started. If not you will need to recognize the running threads between the first two edge stitches. When these stitches are pulled apart, there will be a series of horizontal running strands connecting them.

Note: This cannot be done on pieces that do not have the same number within one or two rows.

a.   Lay out pieces side to side next to each other, right sides facing up, bottom edges toward you. Seam from the bottom edge up.

b.   Thread the strand onto a tapestry needle.

Note: The direction the figure eight is worked depends on which piece the yarn is coming from.

c.   Locate the running thread between the first and second stitch on the bottom row of one piece.

d.   Bring the needle under the thread, picking up the running thread between the first and second stitch on the opposing piece, making a figure eight. (See Fig. 35)

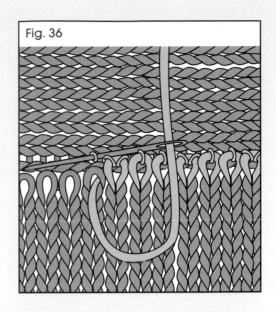

Fig. 36

c.   Go back down into the same stitch and up through the next stitch.

d.   Repeat b–c.

Joining backs to fronts at the shoulder

Joining backs to fronts at the shoulder can be done using the three-needle bind-off method on page 33, grafting method on page 34, and the backstitch on page 36.

Attaching a sleeve to a sweater body

a.   Mark the center of the sleeve cap at the top edge with a safety pin, then align with the shoulder seam on the sweater body. (See Fig. 37)

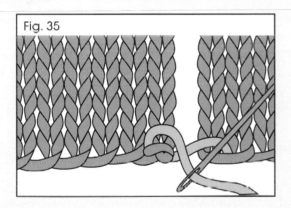

Fig. 35

e.   Work back and forth from running thread to running thread to running thread, keeping the tension easy but firm. Make certain to pull laterally on the seam from time to time. The amount of give should be the same as between two stitches.

Joining stitches head to side

Grafting stitches head to side makes a smooth and weightless seam. You will need to recognize the running thread between the two side stitches then line up the pieces, heads on bottom, and sides above.

a.   With needle and yarn, come up through the first "head" stitch on right or left end of the piece.

b.   Go around the running thread between the first two stitches in the project body. (See Fig. 36)

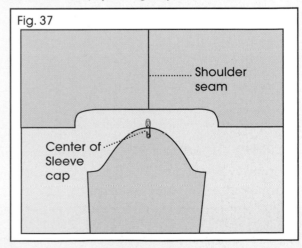

Fig. 37

Shoulder seam

Center of Sleeve cap

b. With right sides facing up, pin the center top of the sleeve cap to the shoulder seam.

c. Line up the bound-off stitches at the beginning of the armhole shaping on both the sleeve and sweater body. Work on only one side at a time. Pin pieces together.

d. Pin the sleeve-cap edge to the armhole at every inch between the bound-off stitches and the shoulder.

e. Use the backstitch or mattress stitch to sew the pieces together along the edge from the bound-off stitches to the shoulder. Pin the other half of the armhole and sleeve in the same manner at the shoulder. Sew from the shoulder to the bound-off stitches.

f. Steam the seam well. Fingerpress seam as the moisture penetrates.

Sewing side and sleeve seams

Making side and sleeve seams can be done using a mattress stitch or backstitch with a tapestry needle.

Mattress stitch
Use a mattress stitch if you have an even number of rows to seam them together.

a. Make a figure eight. Place the two pieces in left hand, without overlapping, and with the two right sides facing you.

b. Pick up strand between first and second stitches on top piece. Pull the yarn.

c. Repeat with lower piece.

d. Repeat b–c. (See Fig. 38)

Both sides must have the same number of rows unless you are gathering one of the sides, or they are in different patterns, or a side selvage is being sewn to a cast-on or bound-off edge. In these cases, pick up two strands instead of one from the appropriate side at regular intervals. Pin if necessary. Bound-off edges can be sewn in the same way, taking one stitch (half if the stitch is large) instead of one strand.

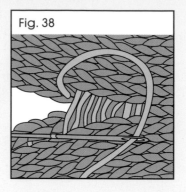
Fig. 38

Backstitch
Backstitch is a strong seam worked from the wrong side of the knitting. One selvage stitch is taken in from each side. Use a backstitch if the front(s) and back have a different number of rows to seam them together.

a. Make a figure eight.

b. Place the two pieces together in left hand, right sides against each other.

c. Insert needle up between first and second row. Pull yarn.

d. Insert needle down between first and cast-on rows, then up between second and third rows. Pull yarn.

e. Repeat d, going down where you first went up, and up one row further to the left. (See Fig. 39)

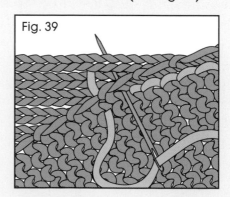
Fig. 39

How do I care for my finished piece?

Cleaning

Most yarn comes with a care label. Please follow the manufacturer's instructions rather than running the risk of ruining your project.

Tips for caring for your knitted projects

• Do not cut snags. Ease the yarn back in position with a tapestry needle.

• Pick off any pills by hand, brush lengthwise with a stiff, dry synthetic sponge or purchase a small fabric shaver.

• Remove stains immediately.

• Wash large items separately.

• Color-test your knitted project by wetting one corner of project and pressing on a white cloth. If it bleeds, use cold water for the first few washes.

• Store knitwear flat in drawer or closed closet, or air-tight container.

• Avoid hanging knitted garments on hangers or hooks.

designed by Colinette Yarns, Ltd.

Section 2: basic techniques

1
technique

What you need to get started:

Knitting needles:
 Size 6 (4.25mm)
Yarn:
 100% mercerized cotton,
 2 oz: red, 1 ball;
 red/black variegated,
 1 ball

How do I cast on, knit, create the garter stitch, and bind off?

This first project will teach you how to cast on stitches (securing the yarn to the needle and creating the first row of knitting), do the knit stitch (the first of two basic stitches used in knitting), create the garter stitch (the pattern formed by the knit stitch when done in both directions), and bind off.

Square Kitchen Cloths

Stitched by Ramona Bryan for the Vanessa-Ann Collection

Skill level: beginner

Finished measurements: 6" square

Here's how:

1. CO 36 sts onto one needle.

CO (Cast On)

a. One yard from the end of the yarn, make a slip knot. (See Fig. 1)

Note: The tail of yarn should be at least three times the width of the edge to be cast on. A longer tail can be cut off, but you may have to start over if your tail is too short.

b. Loop the slip knot onto the needle. (See Fig. 2)

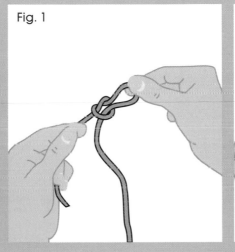

Fig. 1

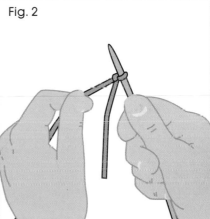

Fig. 2

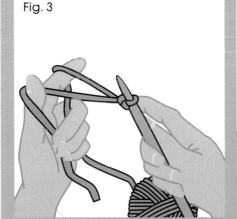

Fig. 3

Fig. 4

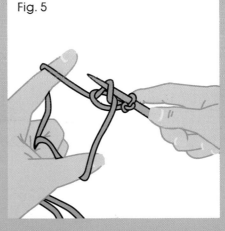

Fig. 5

c. With the needle in the right hand, wrap the tail end of the yarn behind your left thumb. Wrap the yarn from the skein over your left index finger. Hold both yarn ends in your palm. (See Fig. 3)

d. Insert needle tip under the loop on your thumb, then up and over the loop on your index finger. Use needle tip to draw the yarn from the skein through the thumb loop to form a new stitch. (See Fig. 4)

e. Slip thumb out of the loop. Pull tail end of yarn to close the new loop on the needle. (See Fig. 5) Repeat c–e for remaining stitches.

2. K cloth in garter stitch until piece measures 6".

K (knit)

Fig. 1

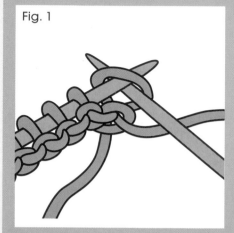

Fig. 2

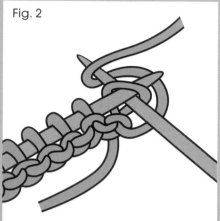

Fig. 3

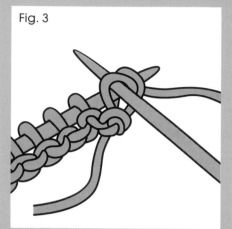

a. Hold needle with cast-on stitches in left hand. Insert tip of right-hand needle into 1st stitch at bottom of left-hand needle, from front to back. The yarn should be waiting at the back of the work. (See Fig. 1)

b. With right index finger, move yarn from skein under, then up and over right-hand needle tip and draw that loop toward you through the original stitch on the left-hand needle. (See Fig. 2)

c. With new loop on the right-hand needle, slip left-hand needle out of the original stitch. (See Fig. 3) Repeat a–c to end of row. When the 1st row is finished, all the stitches will now be on the right-hand needle.

FYI—The first and last stitch on each row create the "selvage" stitches, or side edge stitches.

Garter Stitch

a. Turn work so needle with the stitches is in your left hand again, keeping yarn toward the back. Knit as before to end of row. The pattern formed by the knit stitches done on both sides of the work is called the garter stitch. Continue turning and knitting until piece measures as indicated. After knitting about 4 rows, you will begin to see the horizontal ridges of the garter stitch forming in the work. (See Photo A)

Note: If you put the knitting down and you are in the middle of the row, be certain that when you resume knitting that the yarn is in your right hand and to the back of the row. If you turn it around you will be going back the way you started and will have an uneven row.

Photo A

3. BO all sts.

BO (Bind Off)

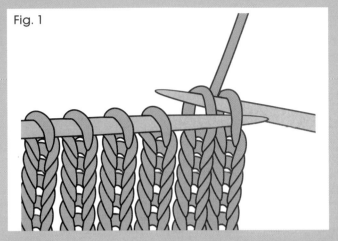

Fig. 1

Fig. 2

a. Hold the needle with the knitting in your left hand, keeping the empty needle and yarn in your right hand. Knit the first 2 stitches in the row. With left-hand needle tip, carefully lift the 1ˢᵗ stitch over the 2ⁿᵈ stitch and off the needle. You should have only 1 stitch on the right-hand needle. (See Fig. 1)

b. Knit the next stitch and lift the previous stitch over the new stitch. (See Fig. 2)

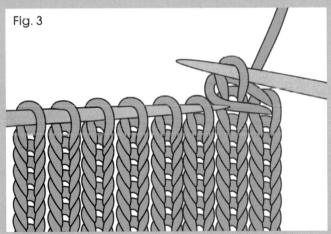

Fig. 3

Fig. 4

c. Continue in this fashion until only one stitch is left on the right-hand needle. (See Fig. 3)

d. Cut yarn, allowing a 6" tail from the completed work. Slip the last stitch off the needle and thread the yarn end through the loop. Pull snugly to secure. (See Fig. 4)

Note: When to bind off will vary with each project.

4. Refer to Blocking on page 32. Block to specified measurements.

5. Refer to Weaving in Yarn Ends & Tails on page 31. Weave in all ends.

What you need to get started:

Knitting needles:
   Size 8 (5mm)
Yarn:
   100% cotton, 84 yds (77m),
   50 gm: blue grey (MC),
   6 balls; chicory (CC),
   1 ball

To make a shape beyond a square, you can either increase or decrease the number of stitches that were orignally cast onto your needle. For this cardigan with raglan sleeves, two methods are used to add onto the original number of stitches—increasing one stitch at a time and casting on an additional number of stitches at the end of a knitted row.

Toddler Cardigan

Designed by Song Palmese

Skill level: beginner

Finished measurements: Child's size 2T, chest: 11", length: 13". Only one size is given; all numbers given refer to the one size. If necessary, adjust needle size to obtain the correct gauge.

Here's how:
Finding the Gauge
1. Refer to Gauge Notation on page 25. Refer to Technique 1, Cast On, Knit, and Garter Stitch on pages 41–42. Using 18 st = 4" with size 8 needles, CO and work in garter stitch to create a gauge swatch.

Knitting the Cardigan Back
2. CO 51 sts with MC. Beg at the waist, work in garter stitch until piece measures 6" (42 rows or 21 ridges).

3. **Armhole shaping:**
   Row 1: K1, inc1, k to 2 sts from the end of the row, inc1, k1.
   Row 2 and all WS rows: K.

Rep these last 2 rows until there are 67 sts total on the right-hand needle. End after a WS row.

45

Inc (increase)

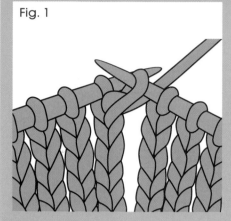

Fig. 1

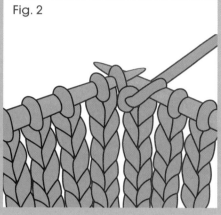

Fig. 2

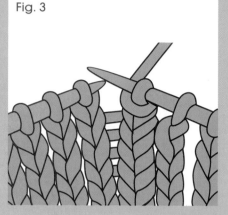

Fig. 3

a. Insert the right-hand needle tip into the front of the stitch and knit it, but do not remove it from the left-hand needle. (See Fig. 1)

b. Insert the right-hand needle tip into the back of the same stitch and knit it again. (See Fig. 2)

c. Move the stitch from the left-hand needle onto the right-hand needle. The new stitch creates a bump on the right side of the work. (See Fig. 3)

4. **Sleeve increases:**
   Cable CO 16 additional sts, k to end of row, Cable CO 16 more sts, k to end of row (99 sts total). Cont in garter stitch until back, from waist to neck, measures 13" (92 rows or 46 ridges).

5. Refer to Technique 1, Bind Off on page 43. BO all sts.

Knitting the Cardigan Front

6. CO 26 sts with MC. Beg at the waist, k in garter stitch until piece measures 6" (42 rows or 21 ridges).

7. **Armhole shaping:**
   Row 1: K1, inc1, k to 1 st from the end of the row, inc1, k1.
   Row 2 and all WS rows: K.

   Rep these last 2 rows until you have 34 sts. End after a WS row.

8. **Sleeve increases:**
   Cable CO 16 additional stitches, k to end of row (50 sts total). K in garter stitch until front, from waist to neck, measures 13" (92 rows or 46 ridges).

9. BO all sts.

10. Repeat Steps 6–9 for other front piece.

Note: Because this piece is worked in garter stitch and the weave is the same on the RS and the WS, you can make two identical pieces. Simply flip one of them when assembling the garment so there is a left front piece and a right front piece.

Knitting the Pocket

11. CO 12 sts with CC. K in garter stitch 24 rows or 12 ridges. BO all sts.

Knitting the Cuffs

12. CO 16 sts with CC. K in garter stitch 64 rows or 32 ridges. BO all sts.

Cable CO (Cable Cast On)

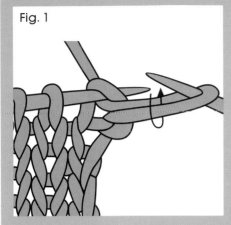

Fig. 1

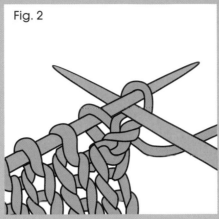

Fig. 2

a. Knit 1ˢᵗ stitch. Do not slip old loop off left-hand needle. Slip new loop onto left-hand needle. (See Fig. 1)

b. Insert the right-hand needle tip between the 2 stitches on left-hand needle. (See Fig. 2)

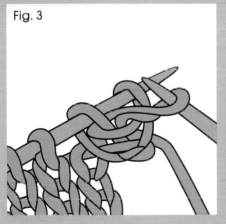

Fig. 3

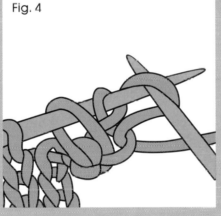

Fig. 4

c. Wrap yarn around right-hand needle tip and bring the new loop through it to the front. (See Fig. 3)

d. Bring new loop to the right and lift it onto left-hand needle. (See Fig. 4) Repeat b–d as indicated.

Finishing the Cardigan

13. Refer to Blocking on page 32. Block all pieces to specified measurements.

14. Refer to Assembling/Sewing Seams on pages 32–36. Center pocket on the left front and sew on.

15. Matching up ridges, sew underarm and side seams together. Matching up top edges, sew top of arms together for 9" from cuff, leaving center 5" of neck unsewn.

16. Using CC, sew blanket stitch around neck, front edges, and bottom edge of sweater. Tack down corners of front for lapel.

17. Using CC, sew each cuff into a tube, then sew one cuff onto each sleeve.

18. Refer to Weaving in Yarn Ends & Tails on page 31. Weave in all ends.

Song Palmese has been working with fiber and bead art for more than 10 years. She began working with beads to keep herself from being bored while employed at an answering-service job.

Once she discovered how to combine the two, knitting and beads, she began to design professionally. Her work has been featured in several knitting magazines and she has been busily gathering some of her favorite designs together for an upcoming line of knitting kits.

Song lives in Oakland, California, with her husband, daughter, and a very bossy guinea pig.

3
technique

What you need to get started:

Knitting needles:
  Size 10.5 (6.5mm)
Yarn:
  100% nylon microfiber,
  88 yds (80m), 50 gm:
  slate blue, 5 balls

How do I purl, create the stockinette stitch, and decrease stitches with knit 2 together method?

This project will teach you how to do the purl stitch (the second of two basic stitches used in knitting) and create the stockinette stitch (the pattern formed by knitting one row and purling the next). It will also teach you how to decrease the number of stitches on your needle, using the "knit 2 together" method.

Child's Cardigan

Designed and stitched by Song Palmese

Skill level: beginner

Finished measurements: Child's size 2T (4T, 6), chest: 28" (30", 32"), length: 15" (16", 17"). If necessary, adjust needle size to obtain the correct gauge.

Here's how:
Finding the Gauge
1. Refer to Gauge Notation on page 25. Refer to Technique 1, Cast On, Knit, and Garter Stitch on pages 41–42. Using 13 st = 4" with size 10.5 needles, CO and work in garter stitch to create a gauge swatch.

3. **Back ribbing:**
P 1 row, then k 1 row to work in stockinette stitch until piece measures 14", (15", 16") from beg. End with a RS row.

P (Purl)

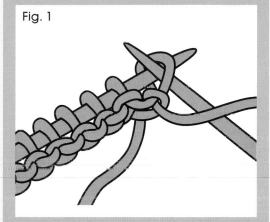

Fig. 1

a. With yarn in front of the work, insert right-hand needle tip into the 1ˢᵗ stitch on the left-hand needle, from back to front. (See Fig. 1)

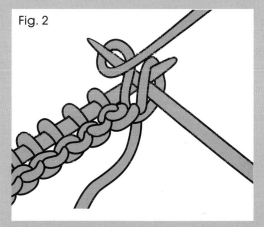

Fig. 2

b. Pull yarn to front of the work, pass it behind and around the right-hand needle tip, and return it to the front of the work. Draw the yarn looped around the right-hand needle through the stitch on the left-hand needle and to back of work. (See Fig. 2)

(continued on page 50)

Knitting the Cardigan Back
2. CO 46 (50, 54) sts. Work 4 rows in garter stitch.

(continued from page 49)

Fig. 3

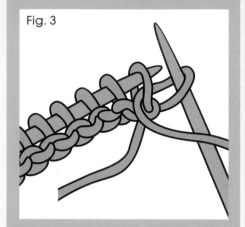

c. With new loop on the right-hand needle, slip left-hand needle out of the original stitch. The new stitch on right-hand needle is a purl stitch. (See Fig. 3) Repeat a–c to end of row.

Stockinette Stitch

Fig. 1

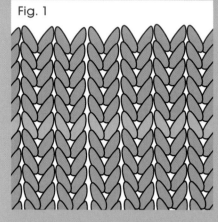

Fig. 2

a. Knit every other row and purl every other row. You will see the knit stitches forming on the RS. (See Fig. 1)

b. You will see the purl ridges on the WS of the work. (See Fig. 2)

Photo A

c. Alternate rows of stitches until knitted piece measures as indicated. (See Photo A)

4. **Neck shaping:**
P14 (16, 18) and k18, p to end of row. K all sts next row (RS). Rep last 2 rows 1 more time. Work should measure 15" (16", 17"). Refer to Technique 1, Bind Off on page 43. BO all sts.

Knit & Purl in the same row

a. After knitting a stitch, bring yarn forward between the needles, ready to purl. (See Fig. 1)

b. After purling a stitch, move yarn between the needles to back of work, ready to knit. (See Fig. 2)

Fig. 1

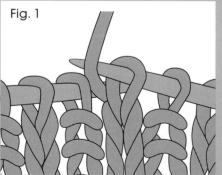

Fig. 2

Knitting the Left Front

5. CO 24 (26, 28) sts. Work 4 rows in garter stitch.

6. **Front ribbing:**
   Beg in stockinette stitch, keeping 4 sts at cardigan front edge in garter stitch and cont until piece measures 11" (12", 13") from beg. End with a WS row.

7. **Neck shaping:**
   <u>Row 1:</u> K18 (20, 22) sts, k2tog, k4.
   <u>Row 2 and WS rows:</u> P.

   Cont in stockinette stitch and maintaining last 4 sts at neck edge in garter stitch, k2tog on every RS row until 14 sts remain. K in patt on rem until piece measures 15" (16", 17") from beg. BO all sts.

Knitting the Right Front

8. Repeat Steps 5–7, working as for left front, but reversing all shaping and patterns and ending with 4 sts in garter stitch.

Knitting the Sleeves

9. CO 20 (22, 24) sts. Work 4 rows in garter stitch.

10. Refer to Technique 2, Increase on page 46.
    Sleeve increases:
    Beg working in stockinette stitch as follows:

    <u>Row 1:</u> K1, inc1, k18, inc1, k1.
    <u>Row 2 and all WS rows:</u> P.

    Cont in stockinette stitch, inc1 st in from both edges every other RS row to equal 40 (42, 44) sts. Work evenly in stockinette stitch until sleeve measures 10" (11", 12"). BO all sts.

K2tog (knit 2 together)

Fig. 1

Note: Knit 2 together is a method for decreasing the number of stitches on your needle that is used for the purpose of shaping a knitted piece. It creates a stitch that slants to the right on the RS.

a. Working on a RS row, bring tip of right-hand needle 2 stitches to the left of the left-hand needle. Insert the right-hand needle tip knitwise into the first 2 stitches on the left-hand needle at the same time.

b. Draw the yarn through to the front of the work, knitting the 2 stitches together as if they were 1 stitch. (See Fig. 1)

FYI—In flat knitting it is very easy to work two identical pieces—such as sleeves—at the same time on the same straight needles. Simply use two balls of yarn.

Work one row on the first piece with one ball of yarn. Then work the same row on the second piece with the second ball of yarn. This method saves a lot of time and ensures that the tension on the two pieces is equal so they will match.

To avoid twisting the two yarns, turn the work clockwise at the end of one row of the pattern, and counterclockwise at the end of the next row.

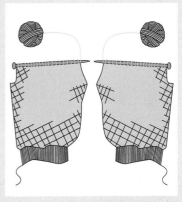

11. Repeat Steps 9–10 for other sleeve.

Finishing the Cardigan

12. Refer to Blocking on page 32. Block all pieces to specified measurements.

13. Refer to Assembling/Sewing Seams on pages 32–36. Sew shoulder seams.

14. Lay back and fronts flat, and mark points 5" (5½", 6") down the sides from the shoulder seams with safety pins. Sew sleeves in between markers, being careful to match center of sleeve with shoulder seams.

15. Sew side and sleeve seams.

16. Refer to Weaving in Yarn Ends & Tails on page 31. Weave in all ends.

How do I decrease with ssk (slip, slip, knit) method and pick up stitches?

This project is a demonstration of symmetry. You will learn how to decrease the number of stitches on your needle with the "slip, slip, knit" method, the mirror of knit 2 together. You will also learn how to add onto a knitted piece by picking up stitches along its vertical edge and along its horizontal edge.

Child's Shell

Designed by Song Palmese

Skill level: advanced beginner

Finished measurements: Sizes 4T (6, 8), chest: 24" (26", 28"), length: 11", 15", 16". All sizes and numbers are given for smallest size, with changes for larger sizes in parentheses. If only one number is given, it applies to all sizes. If necessary, adjust needle size to obtain the correct gauge.

Here's how:
Finding the Gauge
1. Refer to Gauge Notation on page 25. Refer to Technique 1, Cast On and Knit on pages 41–42. Refer to Technique 3, Purl and Stockinette Stitch on pages 49–50. Using 16 sts = 4" with size 8 needles, CO and work in stockinette stitch to create a gauge swatch.

What you need to get started:

Knitting needles:
  Size 6 (4mm)
  Size 8 (5mm)
Yarn:
  50% cotton, 50% acrylic microfiber, 104.5 yds [95m], 50 gm: slate blue 3 (3, 4) balls

Knitting the Back

2. With size 6 needles, CO 49, (53, 57) sts. Work 6 rows in stockinette stitch.

3. Change to size 8 needles and cont in stockinette stitch until piece measures 7½" (8½", 9"), ending with WS row.

4. **Armhole shaping:**
   Refer to Technique 1, Bind Off on page 43. BO 4 sts at the beg of each of the next two rows. Cont in stockinette stitch on the 41 (45, 49) rem until piece measures 13" (14", 15").

5. **Neck shaping:**
   Refer to Technique 3, Knit 2 together on page 51. K13 (14, 16) sts, BO center 15 (16, 17) sts, k to end of row. Knitting with two balls of yarn (joining another piece of yarn for right side), work both sides of back at the same time:

   Left side:
   Row 1 and all odd rows: P.
   Row 2: K10, k2tog, k1.
   Row 4: K9, k2tog, k1.
   Row 5: P. End with 11, (12, 14) sts. BO all sts.

   Right side:
   Row 1 and all odd rows: P.
   Row 2: K1, k2tog, k10.
   Row 4: K1, k2tog, k9.
   Row 5: P. End with 11, (12, 14) sts. BO all sts.

Knitting the Front

6. Knit as for back, repeating Steps 2–4, until piece measures 12", (13", 14").

7. **Neck shaping:**
   K17, (18, 20) sts, BO center 6, (8, 9) sts, k to end of row. Knitting with two balls of yarn, work both sides of front at the same time:

Left front:
Row 1 and all odd rows: P.
Row 2: K14, k2tog, k1.

Cont in stockinette stitch, working k2tog 1 st in from neck edge until there are 11, (12, 14) rem. Cont in stockinette stitch until piece measures 14", (15", 16"). BO all sts.

Right front:
Row 1 and all odd rows: P.
Row 2: K1, ssk, k to end of row.

Cont in stockinette stitch, working SSK 1 st in from neck edge until there are 11, (12, 14) rem. Cont in stockinette stitch until piece measures 14", (15", 16"). BO all sts.

SSK (slip, slip, knit)

a. On knit side, slip 2 stitches from left-hand needle knitwise onto the right-hand needle without knitting them. (See Fig. 1)

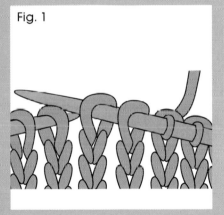
Fig. 1

b. Insert the left-hand needle tip into the front of the loops of these 2 stitches. (See Fig. 2)

c. Wrap the yarn around the right-hand needle tip knitwise and knit the 2 slipped stitches together.

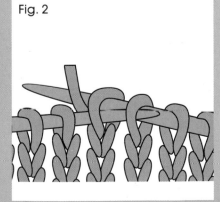
Fig. 2

Note: SSK creates a left-slanting decrease. It is the mirror image of k2tog.

Finishing the Shell

8. Refer to Blocking on page 32. Block all pieces to specified measurements.

9. Refer to Assembling/Sewing Seams on pages 32–36. Sew left shoulder seam.

10. With size 6 needles, and with RS of shell facing you, pick up 64 stitches evenly across neckline. Work 2 rows in stockinette stitch. BO all sts.

11. Sew right shoulder seam and neck seam.

12. With size 6 needles, and with RS of shell facing you, pick up 50 stitches across one armhole. Work 2 rows in stockinette stitch. BO all sts. Repeat for other armhole.

13. Sew side seams.

14. Refer to Weaving in Yarn Ends & Tails on page 31. Weave in all ends.

Pick up Stitches on a horizontal edge

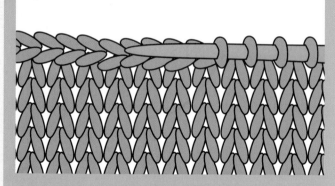

Fig. 1

Note: When you pick up stitches, you start a new skein of yarn. Anchor the yarn to your piece by tying it on or by catching the tail in as you knit the 2nd stitch on this newly formed row.

a. With RS facing you and starting at the right end of the knitted piece, insert the needle tip into the 1st stitch (in the "V") just below the bound-off edge. (See Fig. 1)

Note: Make certain the needle is going into the entire stitch below the bound-off edge.

b. Wrap the yarn around the needle tip knitwise and pull a loop through the stitch.

c. Continue pulling one loop through each stitch across the row.

Pick up Stitches on a vertical edge

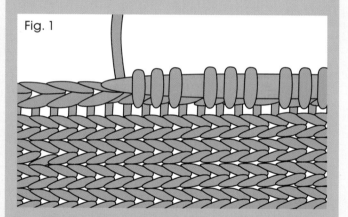

Fig. 1

a. With RS facing you and starting at the right end of the knitted piece, insert the needle tip between the running strands of the first 2 stitches. (See Fig. 1)

b. Wrap the yarn around the needle tip knitwise and pull a loop through.

c. Continue pulling one loop up between the running strands that connect the first 2 stitches along the edge until you have the number indicated.

Note: Because there are more vertical rows of stitches per inch than there are stitches across, make an adjustment when you pick up stitches along a vertical edge. Generally, you want to match stitches to rows. However, to keep the correct ratio of stitches to rows, you should try to skip a running strand interval every few stitches.

What you need to get started:

Knitting needles:
 Four size 8 (5mm)
Yarn:
 100% cotton, 84 yds (77m),
  50 gm: blue grey (MC),
  1 ball; chicory (CC), 1 ball

How do I increase stitches with yarn over method and make eyelets?

Yarn over is a way of making an extra stitch on your needle and creating a deliberate hole, or eyelet, in the fabric. Due to the radical manner in which you are moving the yarn from the back of the work to the front in this method, it is often referred to as "throwing" the yarn.

Baby Booties

Designed by Song Palmese

Skill level: advanced beginner

Finished measurements: Size 6–9 months. Only one size is given; all numbers given refer to one size. If necessary, adjust needle size to obtain the correct gauge.

Here's how:

Finding the Gauge

1. Refer to Gauge Notation on page 25. Refer to Technique 1, Cast On, Knit, and Garter Stitch on pages 41–42. Using 18 st = 4" with size 8 needles, CO and work in garter stitch to create a gauge swatch.

Knitting the Foot

2. Refer to Technique 2, Increase on page 46 and Technique 3, Knit 2 together on page 51. CO 25 sts.
    Row 1: K.
    Row 2: K1, inc1, k8, inc1, k3, inc1, k8, inc1, k1 (29 sts).
    Row 3: K.
    Row 4: K1, inc1, k9, inc1, k1, inc1, k1, inc1, k1, inc1, k9, inc1, k1 (35 sts).
    Rows 5–10: K.
    Row 11: K1, k2tog, k2tog, k25, k2tog, k2tog, k1 (31 sts).
    Row 12: K.
    Row 13: K1, k2tog, k2tog, k21, k2tog, k2tog, k1 (27 sts).
    Row 14: K.
    Row 15: K1, k2tog, k2tog, k17, k2tog, k2tog, k1 (23 sts).

Adding Eyelets

3. Refer to Technique 3, Purl on pages 49–50.
    Row 16: P.

Row 17: K1. *Yo, k2tog; rep from * four times, k4, *yo, k2tog; rep from * to end of row.
Row 18: P.

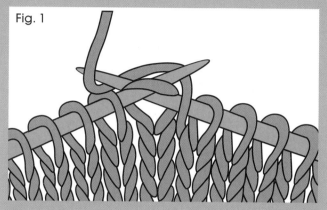

Yo (yarn over)

Fig. 1

a.   Bring yarn forward between the needles into purl position. As you knit the next stitch, the yarn will automatically cross over the right-hand needle, forming a yarn over. (See Fig. 1)

Knitting the Cuff

4. Row 19: *K1, p1; rep from * to end of row.
    Row 20: *P1, k1; rep from * to end of row.
    Rep these 2 rows four more times.

5. Refer to Technique 1, Bind Off on page 43. BO all sts. Cut tail to 24" to sew seam.

Finishing the Bootie

6. Refer to Assembling/Sewing Seams on pages 32–36. Fold knitted piece in half with RS together. With tail, sew seam.

7. Refer to Weaving in Yarn Ends & Tails on page 31. Weave in all ends.

Knitting Ties

8. CO 75 sts with CC. BO all sts.

9. Weave tie through eyelets at ankle of bootie.

How do I change or add colors when knitting?

This project employs three methods for using more than one color in its pattern. First, you will learn how to drop one color and take up the next to work a color block or stripe pattern. Next, you will use the intarsia method to work a motif or area of color. Finally, you will learn how to embroider a motif, using the duplicate stitch method.

Stars & Stripes Baby Sweater

Designed by Karen Baumer

Skill level: advanced beginner

Finished measurements: Size 12 months (24 months), actual chest: 18" (20"), finished chest: 22" (24"). If necessary, adjust needle size to obtain the correct gauge.

Here's how:

Finding the Gauge
1. Refer to Gauge Notation on page 25. Refer to Technique 1, Cast On and Knit on pages 41–42. Refer to Technique 3, Purl and Stockinette Stitch on pages 49–50. Using 20 sts and 28 rows = 4" with size 7 needles, CO and work in stockinette stitch to create a gauge swatch.

Knitting the Sweater Back
2. With size 6 needles and midnight yarn, CO 54 (60) sts. Work 6 rows in stockinette stitch and break yarn. This will create a rolled hem edge.

What you need to get started:

Knitting needles:
    Size 6 (4mm)
    Size 7 (4.5mm)
Yarn:
    100% merino wool, 98 yds, 50 gm: midnight, 1 skein; sand, 2 (3) skeins; wine, 2 skeins

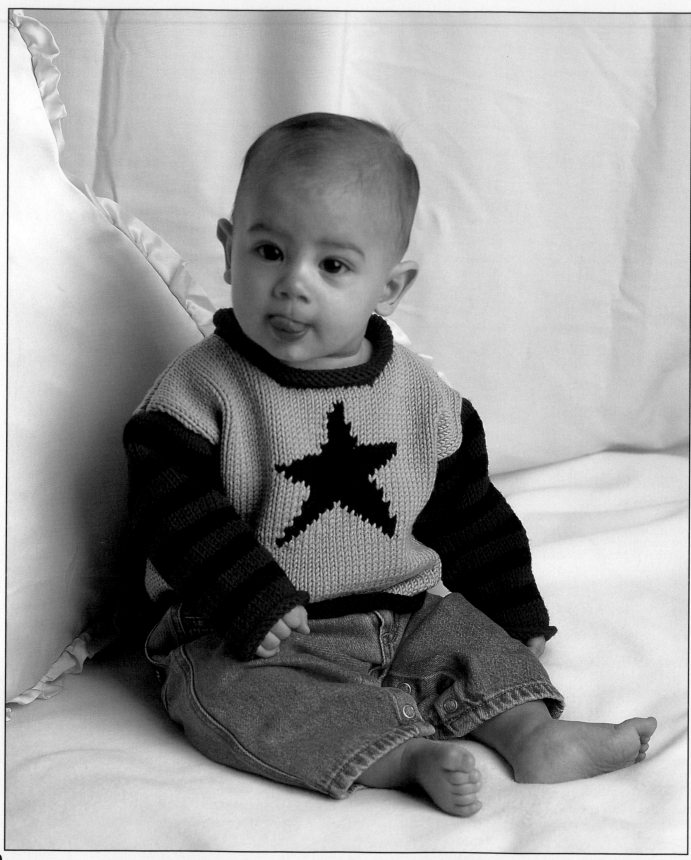

3. Change to size 7 needles and change yarn color to sand.

Change yarn color

a. Insert the right-hand needle tip into the 1st stitch.

b. Drape at least 4" of the tail end of the "new" yarn behind knitted piece.

c. Grab both "old" and "new" yarn strands, twist them together, then work the 1st stitch (the selvage stitch).

d. Drop "old" color and continue on with the "new" color until directed to change again.

4. Work in stockinette stitch until piece measures 5½" (6") from rolled edge of hem (do not unroll edge to measure). End with a WS row.

5. Refer to Technique 1, Bind Off on page 43.
   Armhole shaping:
   BO 2 sts at the beg of the next 2 rows to equal 50 (56) sts.

   Cont in stockinette stitch until piece measures 9½" (10½") from rolled edge of hem, ending with a WS row. BO all sts.

Knitting the Sweater Front

6. Repeat Steps 2–3.

7. Work in stockinette stitch until piece measures 3½" (4") from rolled edge of hem (do not unroll edge to measure). End with a WS row.

8. K17 (20), work intarsia, following Large Star Chart on page 62 and beginning at bottom row— 19 sts—of chart with corresponding colors on bobbins, k18 (21). Cont in stockinette stitch, inserting star motif as established. Remember to measure as you go until piece measures 5½" (6")

from rolled edge of hem (again, do not unroll edge to measure). End with a WS row.

Intarsia

a. Wind two bobbins full of midnight yarn and two bobbins full of sand yarn. Work from the bobbins rather than the whole ball of yarn.

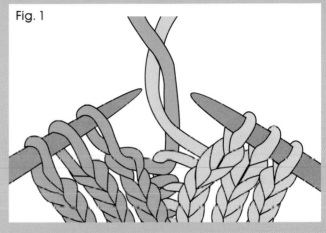
Fig. 1

b. Start at bottom right corner of chart and work left on 1st (RS) row, changing yarn colors as directed. Place the "old" color yarn over the "new" color of yarn at the back of the knitted piece and continue working with the "new" color. (See Fig. 1)

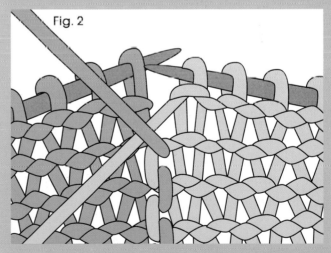
Fig. 2

c. Work next (WS) row to the right. Place the "new" color yarn over the "old" color yarn at the front of the knitted piece and continue working with the "new" color. (See Fig. 2)

(continued on page 62)

(continued from page 61)

Note: On the back of the work, a two-color chain forms where the yarns cross. (See Photo A)

Photo A

Large Star Chart

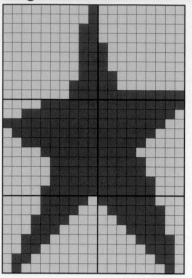

Small Star Chart

12. Rejoin yarn to left side of neck and repeat Step 11 to match other side.

Knitting the Sleeves

13. With size 6 needles and wine yarn, CO 28 (30) sts. Work 4 rows in stockinette stitch. This will create a rolled edge.

9. **Armhole shaping:**
   BO 2 sts at the beg of the next 2 rows to equal 50 (56) sts.

   Cont in stockinette stitch until piece measures 7½" (8½") from rolled edge of hem, ending with a WS row.

10. **Neck shaping:**
    K20 (22), BO center 10 (12) sts, k to end of row.

    Note: From this point, each side of neck is worked separately, beginning with the right side, where yarn is now attached.

11. Work 1 row WS.

    BO 1 st at neck edge on next row and then on every other row three more times to equal 16 (18) sts. When piece measures 9½" (10½") from rolled edge of hem, BO all sts.

14. Refer to Technique 2, Increase on page 46. Change to size 7 needles, cont in stockinette stitch, working Stripe Pattern, changing yarn colors as indicated, and carrying yarn as you go:

Stripe Pattern:
Rows 5–8: wine
Rows 9–12: midnight

Rep these 8 rows, AT SAME TIME, inc in the 1st st at each edge of sleeve starting with the 13th row from beg, then in every 6th row after that five times (starting with the 9th row from beg, then in every 6th row after that seven times) to equal 40 (46) sts. Work evenly until sleeve measures 7" (8") from rolled edge of cuff (do not unroll edge to measure). BO all sts.

Note: You may want to use safety pins or actual row counters to help you keep track of your rows.

Carry yarn as you go

a. After working "first" color, begin working indicated number of rows with "second" color.

b. After working 2 rows in this color, you will arrive at the edge where first color is waiting. As you are about to start the next row with second color, insert the right-hand needle tip into the 1st stitch.

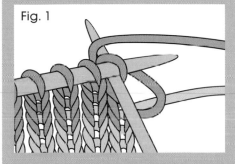
Fig. 1

c. With the working strand (second color) on the left, bring first color up the side. The working strand catches the carried strand. (See Fig. 1)

d. Pick up second color from under first color and make the 1st stitch.

15. Repeat Steps 13–14 for other sleeve.

Embroidering on the Sweater

16. Center and align bottom row of Small Star Chart on page 62 with 4th (5th) row from beg of sand color section on sweater back. With tapestry needle and wine yarn, embroider small star motif, using duplicate stitch.

Duplicate Stitch

a. Bring needle out below and in the center of the stitch that will be covered in duplicate stitch, then bring it around the stitch above it. In the 1st row, work from right to left. If a 2nd row of embroidery is to be worked above that, work that row from left to right. (See Fig. 1)

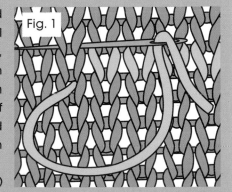
Fig. 1

(continued on page 64)

(continued from page 63)

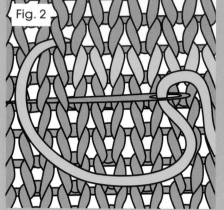

Fig. 2

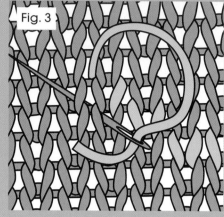

Fig. 3

Fig. 4

b. Insert the needle back into the place where it came out, and bring it out again in the center of the next stitch. After the last duplicate stitch, bring the yarn to the back through the place where it came out, and sew the ends in. (See Fig. 2)

c. When working embroidery stitches on a diagonal, insert needle where it came out before and bring it out again 1 row higher and 1 stitch over to the left or right, as required. (See Fig. 3)

d. When working any vertical embroidery stitches, insert needle where it came out before and bring it out again 1 horizontal strand higher. (See Fig. 4)

Finishing the Sweater

17. Refer to Blocking on page 32. Block all pieces to specified measurements.

18. Refer to Assembling/Sewing Seams on pages 32–36. Sew right shoulder seam.

19. With a safety pin, mark spot on upper back edge where left shoulder seam will meet neck opening.

    Refer to Technique 4, Pick Up Stitches on page 56. With size 6 needles and wine yarn, pick up approximately 58 (62) sts around neck edge as follows: 14 sts along left neck edge, 10 (12) sts across front neck edge, 14 sts along right neck edge, 20 (22) sts along back neck edge, ending at safety pin. Remove safety pin.

    Beg with a purl row, work 7 rows in stockinette stitch. BO all sts loosely.

20. Sew left shoulder and neck seams.

21. Sew tops of sleeves into armhole openings.

22. Sew side seams, reversing seams on rolled edges throughout so that the exposed seams are clean.

23. Refer to Weaving in Yarn Ends & Tails on page 31. Weave in all ends.

Karen Baumer, whose mother taught her to knit at age 14, grew up in San Diego, California. She is now living in Los Angeles.

At her "day job," Karen is the vice president of a small test-development corporation specializing in verbal skills assessment. She has earned graduate degrees in Linguistics and Germanic Literature. Some of her other major interests include gourmet cooking, horses, Italian opera, and Bob Dylan.

How do I decrease stitches with purl 2 together method?

This project teaches you yet another method for decreasing stitches—one that is essential when the pattern requires a decrease on a wrong side row, as this hat does to complete the top shaping. Although the "purl 2 together" method is done on the wrong, or purl, side of the work, it shows itself on the right, or knit, side.

What you need to get started:

Cardboard: 3" x 6"
Craft scissors
Knitting needles:
  Size 6 (4mm)
  Size 7 (4.5mm)
Yarn:
  100% machine washable
    merino wool, 98 yds,
    50 gm: sand, 1 skein;
    wine, 1 skein, midnight,
    1 skein

Stars & Stripes Baby Hat

Designed by Karen Baumer

Skill level: intermediate

Finished measurements: Size 12–24 months, circumference: approximately 18". If necessary, adjust needle size to obtain the correct gauge.

Here's how:

Finding the Gauge

1. Refer to Gauge Notation on page 25. Refer to Technique 1, Cast On and Knit on pages 41–42. Refer to Technique 3, Purl and Stockinette Stitch on pages 49–50. Using 20 sts and 28 rows = 4" with size 7 needles, CO and work in stockinette stitch to create a gauge swatch.

Rows 11–14: sand
Rows 15–18: wine

Rep these 8 rows until the piece measures approximately 5" from bottom rolled edge (do not unroll edge to measure).

4. Refer to Technique 3, Knit 2 together on page 51. **Top shaping:** Cont in stockinette stitch, working Stripe Pattern and starting with a RS row—preferably the 1st row of a stripe:

1st row: *K2, k2tog; rep from * to end of row (60 sts).
2nd row: P.
3rd row: *K2, k2tog; rep from * to end of row (45 sts).
4th row: P.
5th row: *K2, k2tog; rep from * to last stitch, k1 (34 sts).
6th row: P.
7th row: K2tog across (17 sts).
8th row: P2tog across to last stitch, p1 (9 sts).

5. Break yarn, leaving a long tail for sewing.

6. Pull tail firmly through the 9 rem on needle.

Knitting the Hat

2. With size 6 needles and wine yarn, CO 75 sts. Work 10 rows in stockinette stitch, ending with a WS row. This will create a rolled edge.

3. Refer to Technique 2, Increase on page 46 and Technique 5, Change Yarn Color and Carry Yarn as You Go on pages 61 and 63. Change to size 7 needles and change yarn color to sand, cont in stockinette stitch, working Stripe Pattern, inc5 sts in 1st row only, evenly spaced to equal 80 sts, changing yarn colors as indicated and carrying yarn as you go:

P2tog (Purl 2 together)

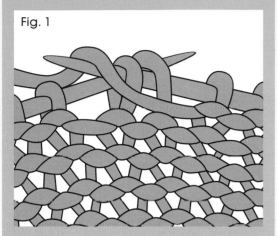

Fig. 1

a. Insert the right-hand needle tip into the front of the next 2 stitches, from left to right. (See Fig. 1) Pull yarn to front of the work and over right-hand needle.

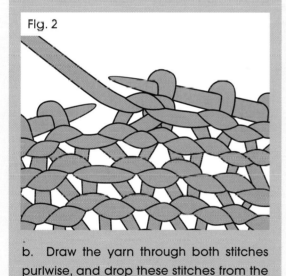

Fig. 2

b. Draw the yarn through both stitches purlwise, and drop these stitches from the needle. (See Fig. 2)

7. Refer to Weaving in Yarn Ends & Tails on page 31. Weave in all ends.

Finishing the Hat

8. Refer to Assembling/Sewing Seams on pages 32–36. Sew back seam, reversing seam on rolled edge so that the exposed seam is clean.

9. With midnight yarn, make a pom-pom.

Make a Pom-pom

a. Using craft scissors, cut two 2¾" circles with a ¾" hole in the center from cardboard. Place them together to form a disk.

b. Double a long strand of yarn on a tapestry needle. Take the needle through the hole, wrap the yarn around outside edge of the disk, and through the hole again. Continue until the entire disk is covered and the hole is nearly filled. (See Fig. 1)

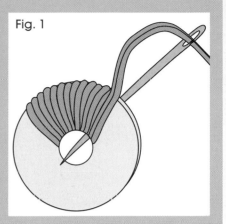

Fig. 1

c. Insert the point of sharp scissors between the two disks at their outer edge and cut the yarn all around. Spread the disks apart slightly. Tightly tie a doubled length of yarn around the center of the yarn between the disks and knot securely. (See Fig. 2)

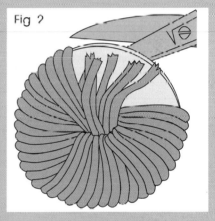

Fig. 2

d. Cut through each disk and remove from yarn. Trim all around the yarn ball (except for the tie yarn lengths) to make it as even as possible. (See Fig. 3)

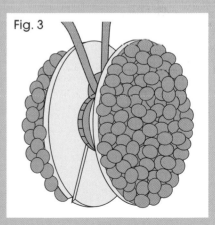

Fig. 3

10. Separately thread each length of yarn used to tie pom-pom onto a tapestry needle, pull through at top of hat to WS of piece, and tie in a square knot. Trim ends.

8
technique

What you need to get started:

Buttons, 4
Knitting needles:
  Size 9 (5.5mm)
  Size 10 (6mm)
Yarn:
  43% wool, 35% acrylic, 22%
    cotton, machine-washable,
    110 yds, 100 gm:
  red (MC), 2 skeins; yellow
  (CC), 1 skein

How do I carry yarn across a row, create a garter ridge pattern, and make buttonholes?

In this pattern, you will work stitches that alternate between two colors in a single row and learn the method for carrying the two yarns across the row. You will then combine rows of garter stitch with rows of stockinette stitch to yield a pattern of ridges in your piece. You will also learn a method for making buttonholes on a buttonhole band.

Yipes! Stripes! Cardigan

Designed by Donna Barnako

Skill level: intermediate

Finished measurements: Child's size 18–24 months (2T, 4T), chest: 12", length: 11". All sizes and numbers are given for smallest size, with changes for larger sizes in parentheses. If only one number is given, it applies to all sizes. If necessary, adjust needle size to obtain the correct gauge.

Here's how:
Finding the Gauge
1. Refer to Gauge Notation on page 25. Refer to Technique 1, Cast On, Knit, and Garter Stitch on pages 41–42. Using 14 sts = 4" with size 9 needles, CO and work in garter stitch to create a gauge swatch.

Knitting the Back

2. Refer to Technique 3, Purl on pages 49–50. Beg with the size 9 needles and MC, CO 40 (44, 48) sts and then work the Corrugated Ribbing Pattern, changing colors as you carry the yarn across the rows as shown on page 70.

Corrugated Ribbing Pattern:

<u>Row 1 (RS):</u> *K2 with MC, twist CC around MC and p2 with CC, rep from * to end of row.

<u>Row 2:</u> *P2 with the MC, twist the CC around MC and k2 with CC, bringing the yarn back to WS and picking up MC so that it twists around CC (to avoid a hole) and rep from * to end of the row.

Rep these 2 rows until there are 4 rows.

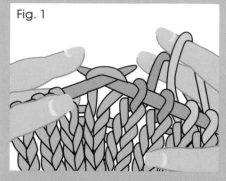

Fig. 1

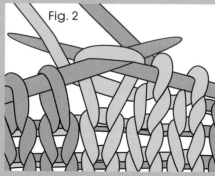

Fig. 2

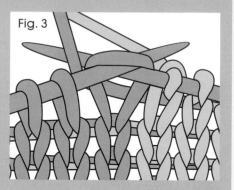

Fig. 3

a. To hold both yarn colors at the same time, hold one color over the index finger and the other color over the middle finger. (See Fig. 1)

b. When working on the RS, hold both colors behind the knitted piece and alternately knit as indicated with the MC yarn... (See Fig. 2)

c. ...and then the CC yarn, bringing it under the MC yarn and up to the needle, making a twist with the two yarns. (See Fig. 3)

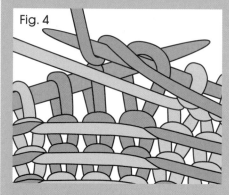

Fig. 4

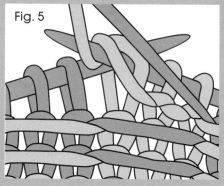

Fig. 5

Photo A

d. On the WS, hold both colors in front of the knitted piece and alternately purl as indicated with the MC yarn... (See Fig. 4)

e. ...and then the CC Yarn. (See Fig. 5)

Note: The resulting loose strands on the WS are called "floats." One color is on top, with the other below it. (See Photo A)

3. Refer to Technique 3, Stockinette Stitch and Knit 2 together on pages 50–51. Change to size 10 needles, beg Garter Ridge Pattern, and dec 1 st by k2tog at the beg of 1st row only:

Garter Ridge Pattern:

Rows 5–8: With MC, work 4 rows in stockinette stitch.

Rows 9–10: Change to CC and k 2 rows to make 1 garter ridge.

Rows 11–16: With MC, work 6 rows in stockinette stitch.

Rows 17–18: Change to CC and k 2 rows to make 1 garter ridge.

Rep these 14 rows until piece measures approximately 10" (12", 14") in length.

4. **Shoulder shaping:**
    Refer to Technique 1, Bind Off on page 43. BO 10 (12, 13) sts at the beg of the next 2 rows. Slip 19 (19, 21) rem onto stitch holder.

Knitting the Right Front

5. Repeat Steps 2–3, but CO 20 (22, 24) sts and work Garter Ridge Pattern until piece measures 2½" less than length of back to shoulders and end with WS row.

6. **Neck shaping:**
BO 7 (7, 8) sts, working rem in Garter Ridge Pattern. Work evenly until piece measures same as back to shoulders, dec 1 st by k2tog at neck edge every RS row two times. BO all sts.

Knitting the Left Front

7. Repeat Steps 5–6, working as for right front, reversing shaping.

Note: You will BO for neck while on a WS row, so end with a RS row at the point of neck shaping.

Knitting the Sleeves

8. Refer to Technique 2, Increase on page 46. Repeat Steps 2–3 on pages 69–70, but CO 24 sts, substituting CC for MC and MC for CC, and inc3 sts across the 1st row only of Garter Ridge Pattern. Cont in Garter Ridge Pattern, inc1 st at each end every 4th row five (seven, nine) times to equal 37 (41, 45) sts. Work evenly until sleeve measures 10" (11", 12") in length. BO all sts.

9. Repeat Step 8 for other sleeve.

Finishing the Cardigan

10. Refer to Blocking on page 32. Block all pieces to specified measurements.

11. Refer to Assembling/Sewing Seams on pages 32–36. Sew shoulder seams.

12. Sew in sleeves, making certain center of sleeve is lined up with shoulder seam.

13. Sew sleeves and side seams.

14. **Left-front Buttonhole Band:**
Refer to Technique 3, Knit 2 together on page 51 and Technique 4, Pick up Stitches on a vertical edge on page 56. With size 9 needles and CC, pick up 26 (34, 42) sts along right front edge and work Corrugated Ribbing Pattern for 4 rows, carrying yarn colors across the rows. Make 4 (5, 6) buttonholes by k2tog at point of buttonhole on 2nd row, then on 3rd row, CO 1 st at buttonhole. BO all sts.

Note: Buttonholes should be on third and fourth stitch from top and bottom of the front, with approximately six stitches separating each, i.e. stitches 3–4, 9–10, 16–17, 23–24 (and 30–31 for size 4; also 37–38 for size 6).

15. **Right-front Button Band:**
With size 9 needles and CC, pick up 26 (34, 42) sts along right front edge and work Corrugated Ribbing Pattern for 4 rows, carrying yarn colors across the rows. BO all sts.

16. **Collar:**
With size 9 needles and CC, and with RS of cardigan facing you, pick up approximately 16 sts from left front edge, 19 (19, 21) sts from back stitch holder, and 16 sts from right front edge. Work 4 rows in garter stitch. BO all sts loosely.

17. Sew buttons onto right-front button band to correspond to buttonhole placement.

18. Refer to Weaving in Yarn Ends & Tails on page 31. Weave in all ends.

Donna Barnako is a knitting teacher, designer, and consultant from Great Falls, Virginia. She organizes and conducts international fiber arts tours and has taken groups to Ireland, New Zealand, Scotland, Wales, Australia, Yorkshire, and Santa Fe.

For 15 years, Donna was the owner/operator of Wooly Knits designer yarn shop in McLean, Virginia. She has been a knitter for four decades and in her "previous life" she was a lobbyist for the health care industry.

Circular knitting needles:
Size 6 (4mm) 16"
Size 8 (5mm) 16"
Double-pointed knitting
needles: Size 8, set of 4
Yarn:
2-ply worsted wool, 210 yd,
4 oz: ecru, 1 skein; green,
1 skein; red, 1 skein

How do I knit in the round, using circular and double-pointed knitting needles?

Knitting in the round allows you to create a seamless tube, such as required by a stocking, hat, or pair of mittens, by knitting round and round in a spiral with the right side always facing you. Knitting a colored pattern like this one is easy in the round as you can always see the right side of the fabric.

Moose Christmas Stocking

Designed by Anne Maillette

Skill level: intermediate

Finished measurements: 7" x 22". If necessary, adjust needle size to obtain the correct gauge.

Here's how:

Notes: The stocking will be knit in the round from the top down to the toe. To this point, you are familiar with working rows in flat knitting. In circular knitting, you work rounds.

To begin knitting on circular needles, cast on as you would on a straight needle. Make certain that cast-on stitches are not twisting around the needle. The yarn end will be on the right-hand needle. To join, simply knit into the first cast-on stitch.

To work stockinette stitch in the round, simply knit. For garter stitch in the round, alternately work one round in knit and one round in purl.

To begin knitting on double-pointed needles, first cast on stitches onto a straight needle of the same size. If you are changing from circular needles to double-pointed needles, carefully remove the circular needles from your piece. Then, while working at a table, slide the stitches purlwise onto your double-pointed needles, distributing them as indicated or in amounts as equal as possible. You will be able to form a triangle with three needles.

You will need a fourth double-pointed needle for knitting. Again make certain that cast-on stitches are not twisting around the needles. The first few rows of knitting will be awkward to work with, but as the piece grows, the weight of it will help keep the needles balanced and in place.

Finding the Gauge

1. Refer to Gauge Notation on page 25. Refer to Technique 1, Cast On, and Knit on pages 41–42. Using 16 sts = 4" with size 8 circular needles, create a gauge swatch as follows:

CO and k 1 row. Break the yarn, slide the knitting, with the RS facing, back to the knitting end of the needle, and k another row. Break the yarn again and repeat so all rows are worked from the RS.

Note: This method will create stockinette stitch.

Knitting the Hem (Rounds 1–12)

2. With size 6 circular needles and green yarn, loosely CO 54 sts.

Note: These cast-on stitches will be used later to create the hem.

3. Place a row marker on right-hand needle. Join yarn with 1st st on left-hand needle (bringing the 1st and last cast-on stitches together to form the circle of stitches) by knitting into it, being careful not to twist cast-on stitches. K 11 rounds.

Note: The row marker serves to alert you to the beginning of the round. Slip marker from one needle tip to the other when you come to it.

4. Refer to Technique 4, Pick up Stitches on a horizontal edge on page 56. On round 12, pick up 1st cast-on stitch with left-hand needle with WS facing each other. K tog first 2 sts (cast-on stitch plus 1st knit stitch) on left-hand needle. Complete round 12, picking up the corresponding cast-on stitch and k it tog with the next knit stitch.

Note: Here, the 11 rounds you have completed are doubled-over to create a hem that is approximately six rounds tall.

Knitting the Leg (Rounds 13–78)

5. Refer to Technique 6, Change Yarn Color and Carry Yarn as You Go on pages 61 and 63. Change to size 8 circular knitting needles and ecru yarn. K 12 rounds.

   Note: This is where you will later personalize the stocking.

6. Refer to Technique 8, Carry Yarn Across on page 70. Change to red yarn and follow Moose Christmas Stocking Chart on page 76, beg with round 25 through round 78, changing yarn colors as indicated. At end of round 78, break ecru yarn.

Knitting the Heel Marker (Rounds 79–80)

7. K with green yarn as chart indicates up until the last 13 sts. With a scrap of ecru yarn, k the last 13 sts and 13 sts of the next round (26 sts). With the left-hand needle, pick up and transfer these 26 sts back onto the left-hand needle. (This 26-stitch stripe will be removed later to set in the heel.) Reknit these 26 sts with green yarn and complete round 80.

Knitting the Foot (Rounds 81–110)

8. Cont, following Moose Christmas Stocking Chart.

Knitting the Toe

9. Change to red yarn and work 1 round, dec 2 sts evenly spaced by k2tog (52 sts).

10. Refer to Technique 3, Knit 2 together on page 51. **Shaping round:**

    K10, k2tog, k2, sl1, k1, psso, k20, k2tog, k2, sl1, k1, psso, k10. K 1 round. Cont to dec 4 sts by k2tog and psso every other round until there are 16 rem. (Change to double-pointed needles when necessary.) Break yarn, leaving 12" tail.

Sl (Slip)

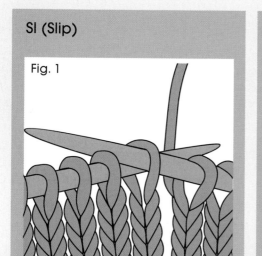

a. Insert the right-hand needle tip purlwise into the first stitch on the left-hand needle and slip it off the left-hand needle onto the right-hand needle without knitting it or changing its orientation. (See Fig. 1)

Psso (Pass slipped stitch over)

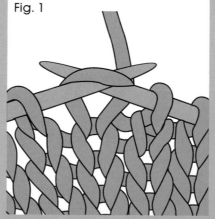
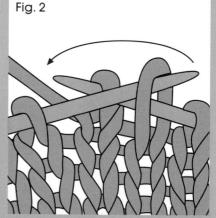

a. Slip the first stitch knitwise onto the right-hand needle. (See Fig. 1)

b. Knit the next stitch and pass the slipped stitch over it. (See Fig. 2)

Note: This stitch creates a single decrease that slants to the left. It is often paired with k2tog.

11. With a tapestry needle, weave tail through the 16 rem. Draw tight and secure on inside of toe.

Knitting the Heel

12. With a double-pointed needle, pick up 26 green sts below scrap yarn. With a second double-pointed needle, pick up 26 sts above scrap yarn. Carefully pick out scrap yarn stripe, opening up 52 sts.

13. Divide sts onto three double-pointed needles as follows:
Needle 1 (beginning at side opening): 18 sts;
Needle 2: 8 sts, place marker (at opposite side opening), 8 sts;
Needle 3: 18 sts.

Beginning at marker, join a new red yarn and work 1 round.

14. **Shaping round:**
K1, sl1, k1, psso, k20, k2tog, k2, sl1, k1, psso, k20, k2tog, k1. K 1 round. Cont to dec 4 sts by k2tog and psso every other round until there are 20 rem.

15. Refer to Assembling/Sewing Seams on pages 32–36. Divide rem evenly onto two needles. Sew edges together.

Finishing the Stocking

16. Turn stocking inside out. Refer to Weaving in Yarn Ends & Tails on page 31. Weave in all ends.

17. To make hand loop, cut a strand of green yarn approximately 2 yds in length. Using a crochet hook, chain a 4" length, leaving a 4" tail. Separately thread each yarn tail onto a tapestry needle, pull through inside of the stocking at center back, and tie in a square knot. Weave in ends.

Crochet a Chain

a. Make a slip knot on the crochet hook as you would to cast onto a knitting needle.

b. Holding the hook like a pencil in your right hand and the yarn between the thumb and middle finger of your left hand, wrap the yarn up and over the hook (from back to front). (See Fig. 1)

Fig. 1

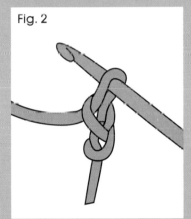
Fig. 2

Fig. 3

c. Using hook, pull the yarn through the loop already on the hook. (See Fig. 2)

d. Repeat b–c to desired length. (See Fig. 3) Cut yarn and pull through the loop.

18. Refer to Technique 6, Duplicate Stitch on pages 63–64. To personalize your stocking, use the Moose Christmas Stocking Alphabet Chart on page 77 to help you lay out your personalization. With tapestry needle and red yarn, stitch the letters in duplicate stitch within the ecru band at the top of the stocking.

FYI—When working colors where more than one ball or bobbin of yarn is used, keep yarns separated somehow, either in dedicated containers or to the right and left of your lap. Always twist yarns only to prevent holes. Always turn the work so that tangles untwist rather than twisting further.

Moose Christmas Stocking Chart

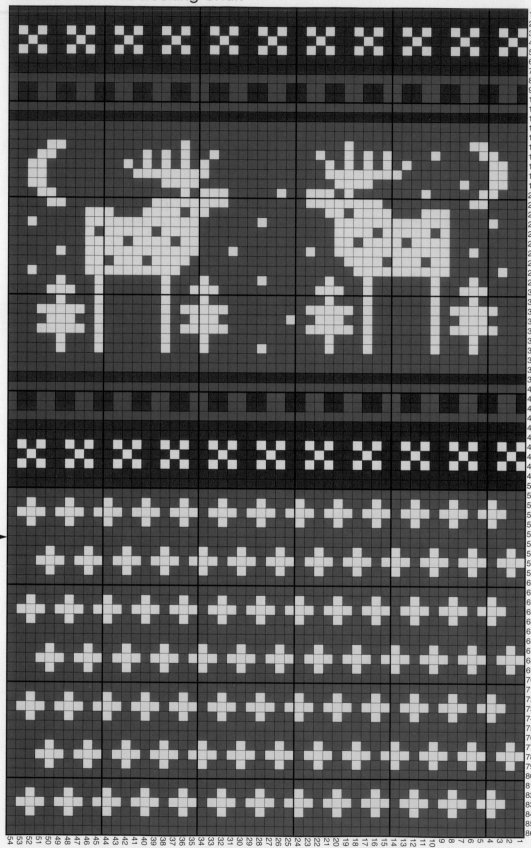

Insert
Heel
Marker→

76

Moose Christmas Stocking Alphabet Chart

Section 3: beyond the basics

How do I make a simple embellishment?

What you need to get started:

Knitting needles:
   Size 6 (4mm)
Yarn:
   50% wool, 50% cotton,
      123 yds, (113m), 50 gm:
      rose, 1 skein

This project set provides two different types of embellishments. Either can easily be tacked onto any project. The flower, made up of individual shaped petals, is an ornament that can sit sweetly on top of the Eyeleted Baby Hat on page 84, while the heart is an appliqué that is quite charming when sewed onto the Toddler Cardigan on page 44.

Simple Embellishments

See "Flower" photo on page 79, bottom right.
See "Heart" photo on page 78, top left.

Designed by Song Palmese

Skill level: advanced beginner

Finished measurements: Flower is 3"–4" across, rolled into a cone. Heart is 4" x 3". If necessary, adjust needle size to obtain the correct gauge.

Here's how:
Finding the Gauge
1. Refer to Gauge Notation on page 25. Refer to Technique 1, Cast On and Knit on pages 41–42 and Technique 3, Purl and Stockinette Stitch on pages 49–50. Using 22 sts = 4" with size 6 needles, CO and work in stockinette stitch to create a gauge swatch.

Knitting the Flower Petals
2. CO 2 sts.

3. Refer to Technique 2, Increase on page 46. Work as follows:

Row 1 and all WS rows: P.
Row 2: Inc1, k1 (3 sts).
Row 4: Inc1, inc1, k1 (5 sts).
Row 6: Inc1, k2, inc1, k1 (7 sts).
Row 8: Inc1, k4, inc1, k1 (9 sts).
Row 10: K.

4. Break yarn, but leave flower petal on needle.

5. Repeat Steps 2–4 for five more petals. At the end of the 6th petal, do not break yarn.

6. Refer to Technique 3, Knit 2 together on page 51. K across all six petals on needle:

Row 1 and all WS rows: P.
Row 2: *K1, k2tog; repeat from * to end of row.

Rep these 2 rows until there are 16 rem. End with WS row.

Next row: *K2tog; repeat from * to end of row.
Next row: P.

Rep these 2 rows until there are 4 rem.

Finishing the Flower

7. Refer to Technique 1, Bind Off on page 43. BO all sts and break yarn, leaving 12" tail for sewing flower together and tacking it down.

8. Refer to Blocking on page 32. Block all pieces to specified measurements.

9. Refer to Weaving in Yarn Ends & Tails on page 31. Weave in all ends, except for tail.

10. Curl flower up into cone shape and move petals until satisfied with flower shape. Using long tail, sew flower together.

Knitting the Heart

1. CO 1 st.

2. Refer to Technique 2, Increase on page 46. Work increases as follows:

Row 1: Inc1.
Row 2: Inc1, k1.
Row 3: Inc1, k2.

Cont in this manner, inc1 st at the beg of each row until there are 15 sts.

3. Refer to Technique 3, Knit 2 together on page 51. Dec for lobes:

1st dec row: K2tog, k4, k2tog.
2nd row: K.
3rd row: K2tog, k to 2 sts from end, k2tog.

Finishing the Heart

4. Refer to Technique 1, Bind Off on page 43. BO all sts and break yarn.

5. Rejoin yarn at center of heart, rep from 1st dec row to BO, using center st for both lobes.

6. Refer to Blocking on page 32. Block to specified measurements.

7. Refer to Weaving in Yarn Ends & Tails on page 31. Weave in all ends.

Tips

This flower can be made larger or smaller by increasing to different numbers of stitches.

The heart also can be made larger or smaller by increasing to different numbers of stitches, as long as there are an odd number when the lobes are started.

Try making one or both of these embellishments in a different yarn for a different look, texture, and size.

What you need
to get started:

Knitting needles:
   Size 6 (4mm), 20" long
Yarn:
   100% acrylic, 5 oz (140 gm):
   pale blue, 1 ball

How do I create a seed stitch pattern and a basket-weave pattern?

This project presents two popular patterns. The seed stitch, made up of a combination of alternating single knit and purl stitches, yields a highly textured pattern. The basket-weave pattern, which develops as a number of knit stitches alternate with a number of purl stitches over a series of eight rows, creates the illusion of a woven piece of cloth.

Bassinet Blanket

Stitched by Ann Schuman for the Vanessa-Ann Collection

Skill level: advanced beginner

Finished measurements: 26" x 23". If necessary, adjust needle size to obtain the correct gauge.

Here's how:
Finding the Gauge
1. Refer to Gauge Notation on page 25. Refer to Technique 1, Cast On and Knit on pages 41–42 and Technique 3, Purl and Stockinette Stitch on pages 49–50. Using 20 sts and 28 rows = 4" with size 6 needles, CO and work in stockinette stitch to create a gauge swatch.

Knitting the Blanket
2. CO 102 sts.

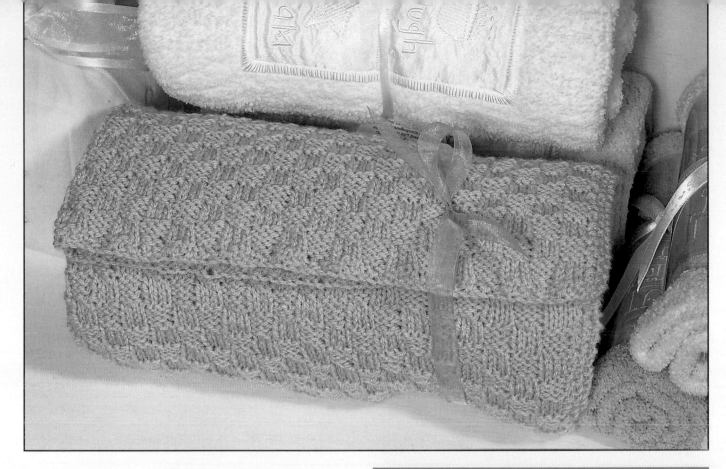

3. Work 3 rows in seed stitch. Place a stitch marker.

4. Work Basket-weave Pattern as follows:

    Basket-weave Pattern:
    <u>1st–4th rows:</u> K1, p1, k1, * K3, p3, rep from * to
    last 3 sts, place stitch marker, k1, p1, k1.
    <u>5th–8th rows:</u> K1, p1, k1, *P3, k3, rep from * to
    last 3 sts, k1, p1, k1.

    Rep these 8 rows until piece measures 22½".

5. Repeat Step 3 without placing a stitch marker.

6. Refer to Technique 1, Bind Off on page 43. BO
    all sts.

Finishing the Blanket

7. Refer to Blocking on page 32. Block to specified
    measurements.

8. Refer to Weaving in Yarn Ends & Tails on page 31.
    Weave in all ends.

Seed Stitch

a. On every other row, beginning with a RS row, knit
one stitch, then purl one stitch, making certain to
pass yarn between—not over—needles, to end
of row.

b. On every other row, beginning with a WS row,
purl one stitch, then knit one stitch to end of row.

c. Continue to alternate rows of stitches until knitted
piece measures as indicated. (See Photo A)

Photo A

Circular knitting needles:
   Size 8 (5mm), 16"
Double-pointed knitting
   needles: Size 8, set of 4
Yarn:
   100% cotton, 84 yds (77m),
   50 gm: chicory, 1 ball

How do I combine flat knitting with knitting in the round?

Switching from flat knitting to knitting in the round is relatively easy, given the right project. The eyeleted edge on this hat is worked on circular knitting needles in flat knitting and then the seam is sewed up later. The work is joined into a circle for knitting the body of the hat in the round and double-pointed knitting needles are used to shape the top.

Eyeleted Baby Hat

Designed by Song Palmese

Skill level: advanced beginner

Finished measurements: Size 6–9 months, circumference: approximately 18". Only one size is given; all numbers given refer to one size. If necessary, adjust needle to obtain the correct gauge.

Here's how:

Note: Lace edging is knit flat, then edging is joined into circle and hat is knitted in the round.

Finding the Gauge

1. Refer to Gauge Notation on page 25. Refer to Technique 1, Cast On and Knit on pages 41–42. Using 18 sts = 4" with size 8 needles, create a gauge swatch as follows:

stitches on the needle. If necessary, take the time to correct their orientation.

5. K every round until hat is 5" from point where you began knitting in the round.

6. **Top shaping:**
Change to double-pointed needles and begin decreases:

<u>1st round:</u> *K6, k2tog, rep from * to beg of round (56 sts).
<u>2nd round:</u> K 1 round.
<u>3rd round:</u> *K5, k2tog, rep from * to beg of round (48 sts).
<u>4th round:</u> K 1 round.
<u>5th round:</u> *K4, k2tog, rep from * to beg of round (40 sts).
<u>6th round:</u> *K3, k2tog, rep from * to beg of round (32 sts).
<u>7th round:</u> *K2, k2tog, rep from * to beg of round (24 sts).
<u>8th round:</u> *K1, k2tog, rep from * to beg of round (16 sts).
<u>9th round:</u> K2tog all the way around (8 sts).
<u>10th round:</u> K2tog all the way around (4 sts).

Finishing Hat

7. Break yarn, leaving a 6" tail.

8. Using tapestry needle, draw tail tightly through all stitches on double-pointed needles. Remove double-pointed needles. Pull yarn tightly (pull through twice if necessary), and weave in end to close edge.

9. Refer to Assembling/Sewing Seams on pages 32–36. Sew seam of lace edging on reverse side so that the exposed seam is clean.

10. Refer to Weaving in Yarn Ends & Tails on page 31. Weave in all ends.

11. Fold edging up over bottom of hat.

CO and k 1 row. Break yarn, slide the knitting, with the RS facing back to the knitting end of the needle, and k another row. Break the yarn again and repeat so all rows are worked from the RS.

Knitting Lace Edging

2. With circular needles, CO 64 sts.

3. Refer to Technique 3, Purl and Knit 2 together on pages 49–51, Technique 5, Yarn Over on page 58, and Technique 4, Slip, Slip, Knit on page 55. Work in flat knitting as follows:

<u>Row 1:</u> P.
<u>Row 2:</u> *K1, k2tog, k1, yo, k1, yo, k1, ssk, rep from * seven times.
<u>Row 3:</u> P.
<u>Rows 4–7:</u> Rep Rows 2–3 two times.
<u>Row 8:</u> K.

Knitting Hat

4. Place a stitch marker on right-hand needle. Join stitches into circle, being careful not to twist

Double-pointed knitting
    needles: Size 2 (2.75mm)
    [5 (3.75mm)], set of 4
Knitting needles:
    Size 2 (2.75mm) [3 (3mm);
    5 (3.75mm); 7 (4.5mm)]
Polyester stuffing
Silk leaves (optional)
Yarn:
    Any sport [double knitting;
    worsted; or bulky] weight:
    pumpkin, approx. 25 yds
    Any sport or double
    knitting [worsted] weight:
    brown, small amount

How do I knit a sphere?

In this project, you will knit seven wedges that are shaped by slipping a different number of stitches at the beginning and end of each row. When these wedges are grafted together, they form a sphere that is perfectly suited to molding into a pumpkin.

Pumpkin Ornament

Designed by Janet Rehfeldt

Skill level: advanced beginner

Finished measurements: Determined by the size needles and weight of yarn used. Use size 2 for sport weight; size 3 for double knitting weight; size 5 for worsted weight; or size 7 for bulky yarn.

Here's how:
Note: Gauge is not important.

Knitting the Pumpkin Body

1. Refer to Technique 1, Cast On on page 41. With straight knitting needles and pumpkin yarn, CO 18 sts.

2. Refer to Technique 1, Knit on page 42 and Technique 9, Slip on page 74. K 1 row. Work patt as follows:

    Row 1: Sl1, k16, sl1.
    Row 2: Sl2, p14, sl2.
    Row 3: Sl3, k12, sl3.
    Row 4: Sl4, p10, sl4.
    Row 5: Sl5, k8, sl5.

    Row 6: Sl6, p6, sl6.
    Row 7: Sl7, k4, sl7.
    Row 8: Sl6, p6, sl6.
    Row 9: Sl5, k8, sl5.
    Row 10: Sl4, p10, sl4.
    Row 11: Sl3, k12, sl3.
    Row 12: Sl2, p14, sl2.
    Row 13: Sl1, k16, sl1.
    Row 14: K18.

3. Refer to Technique 1, Bind Off on page 43. BO all sts to complete one wedge of the pumpkin.

4. Repeat Steps 1–3, working patt from Rows 1–14 five more times, then from Rows 1–13 once for a total of seven wedges.

Assembling the Pumpkin

5. Refer to Assembling/ Sewing Seams on pages 32–36. Graft together the cast-on and bound-off ends of the body to form a ball, making certain that each graft leaves a purl ridge for matching the other sections of the body.

Knitting the Stem

6. Refer to Technique 3, Knit 2 together on page 51. **In the round:** With brown yarn and double-pointed needles, pick up and k16 sts around one open end of the pumpkin body. Place a marker (16 sts).

Round 2: *K2tog, rep from * around (8 sts).
Rounds 3–4: Work even.
Round 5: Rep Round 2 (4 sts).

7. Break yarn, leaving a 6" tail.

8. Using tapestry needle, draw tail tightly through 4 sts on double-pointed needles. Remove double-pointed needles. Pull yarn tightly, and weave in end to close edge and form top of stem.

Finishing the Pumpkin

9. Stuff pumpkin with polyester stuffing, filling short-rowed areas firmer to form pumpkin ridges. Thread a running stitch around remaining open end of body and pull tightly to close. Shape your pumpkin to resemble a real pumpkin.

10. Decorate with a silk leaf at the base of the stem if desired.

Janet Rehfeldt has been knitting and crocheting since she was seven years old. She owns a small business called Knitted Threads Designs, which she operates with her mother. Their designs have been featured in various magazines and several chapter newsletters.

Janet teaches and conducts workshops for local guilds and yarn shops as well as participating in national conferences.

Janet lives in Sun Prairie, Wisconsin, with her husband, their Golden Retriever, and two cats.

What you need to get started:

Double-pointed knitting
   needles: Size 3 (3 mm),
   7" long, set of 4
Knitting needles:
   Size 3 (3 mm)
Yarn:
   2-ply worsted wool, 210 yd,
   4 oz: red-blue tweed,
   1 skein

How do I knit an entire garment in one piece?

The body of this sweater is knit in one continuous piece, using straight knitting needles and working in flat knitting. The turtleneck is added on later and worked in the round with double-pointed needles.

Mini Sweater

Designed by the Vanessa-Ann Collection

Skill level: advanced beginner

Finished measurements: 8½" x 5". If necessary, adjust needle size to obtain the correct gauge.

Here's how:
Finding the Gauge
1. Refer to Gauge Notation on page 25. Refer to Technique 1, Cast On and Knit on pages 41–42. Refer to Technique 3, Purl and Stockinette Stitch on pages 49–50. Using 20 sts and 28 rows = 4" with size 3 needles, CO and work in stockinette stitch to create a gauge swatch.

Knitting the Back
2. With knitting needles, CO 19 sts. Work ribbing as follows:

   Row 1: *K1, p1, rep from * to end of row.
   Row 2: *P1, k1, rep from * to end of row.
   Rows 3–5: Rep Rows 1 and 2, alternating and ending with RS row.
   Row 6: K to end of row.
   Row 7: P to end of row.
   Rows 8–18: Rep Rows 6 and 7, alternating and ending with WS row.

Knitting the Neck

8. Refer to Technique 4, Pick up Stitches on a horizontal edge on page 56. With RS facing you, divide sts evenly onto three double-pointed needles to work in rounds, join yarn to left shoulder, pick up and k7 sts to front, k5 sts from stitch holder, pick up and k7 sts to right shoulder, pick up and k9 sts across back (28 sts).

9. Work neck ribbing in rounds as follows:
Rounds 1–10: *K1, p1, rep from * around.
BO all sts loosely.

Knitting the Cuffs

10. With RS facing you, join yarn to 1st st, work along side edge of one sleeve, pick up and k1 st in every other st across (14 sts).

11. Work cuff ribbing as follows:
Rows 1–5: *K1, p1, rep from * to end of row.
BO all sts.

12. Repeat Steps 10–11 for other sleeve.

Finishing the Sweater

13. Refer to Assembling/Sewing Seams on pages 32–36. Sew sleeves and side seams.

14. Refer to Weaving in Yarn Ends & Tails on page 31. Weave in all ends.

Knitting the Sleeves

3. Work sleeves as follows:

Row 19: P to end of row. Cable CO 10 sts (29 sts).
Row 20: K to end of row. Cable CO 10 sts (39 sts).
Row 21: P to end of row.
Rows 22–27: Cont in stockinette stitch for 6 rows.

4. **Neck shaping:**
Row 28: K17, slide next 5 sts onto a stitch holder, join another piece of yarn for right side, k17.

5. Refer to Technique 3, Knit 2 together on page 51 and Technique 7, Purl 2 together on page 67. Knitting with two balls of yarn, work both sides at the same time, reversing shaping on the left side:

Shoulder & Top of Sleeve:
Row 29: P15, p2tog.
Row 30: K2tog, k14.
Row 31: P15.
Row 32: K15.
Row 33: P15. Break yarn.

Knitting the Front

6. Work as follows:

Row 34: K15, CO 9 (neck), k15.
Row 35: P (39 sts).
Rows 36–43: Work in stockinette stitch for 8 rows.

7. Refer to Technique 1, Bind Off on page 43. Work as follows:

Row 44: BO 10 sts, k29.
Row 45: BO 10 sts, p19.
Rows 46–59: Work in stockinette stitch for 14 rows.

6
project

What you need to get started:

Buttons, 2

Knitting needles:

   Size 10 (6mm)

Yarn:

   1st (bouclé) bulky weight (43% kid mohair, 32% lamb's wool, 20% silk, 5% nylon), 60 yds [48m], 48 gm: olive/taupe/chartreuse/plum variegated, 5 (6, 6, 6) skeins

   2nd (hairy) bulky weight (43% kid mohair, 32% lamb's wool, 20% silk, 5% nylon), 60 yds [48m], 48 gm: olive/taupe/chartreuse/plum variegated, 5 (5, 6, 6) skeins

   Worsted weight (45% silk, 45% kid mohair, 10% lamb's wool), 110 yds [100 m], 50 gm: olive/taupe/chartreuse/plum variegated, 5 (5, 6, 6) skeins

How do I knit a piece with a diagonal weave?

Although it is worked entirely in garter stitch, this mid-hip length jacket is quite interesting with its diagonal panels, cutouts, and back slit. The back is made up of two diagonal-slanting pieces with a belt loop over the back slit. Tie closures are used on the front and accent the collar which is folded over on one side and V-shaped on the other.

Origami Jacket

Designed by Donna Barnako

Skill level: advanced beginner

Finished measurements: Bust: small 36"; (medium 40"; large 44"; extra large 48") Length: 22" (24", 24", 24"). If only one figure appears within parentheses, it applies to sizes medium through extra large. If necessary, adjust needle size to obtain the correct gauge.

Here's how:

Finding the Gauge

1. Refer to Gauge Notation on page 25. Refer to Technique 1, Cast On, Knit, and Garter Stitch on pages 41–42. Using 13.6 sts and 28 rows = 4" with size 10 needles, CO and work in garter stitch to create a gauge swatch.

Knitting the Right Front

2. Refer to Technique 6, Change Yarn Color and Carry Yarn as You Go on pages 61 and 63. With size 10 needles and 1st bulky-weight yarn, CO 30 (34, 38, 42) sts. K 1 row. Change to worsted-weight

Repeat these 8 rows until piece measures 22" (24", 24", 24").

3. Refer to Technique 1, Bind Off on page 43. BO all sts loosely.

Knitting the Left Front

4. Refer to Technique 2, Increase on page 46. With size 10 needles and 1st bulky-weight yarn, CO 15 sts. K 1 row. Change to worsted-weight yarn and beg working Color Pattern at Row 5. AT THE SAME TIME, inc in the 1st and last stitch of this row and every other row, working patt and changing yarns until horizontal measurement of piece is approximately 9" (10", 11", 12") (49 sts for medium). Note on paper the number of stitches for your piece. (See Fig. 1)

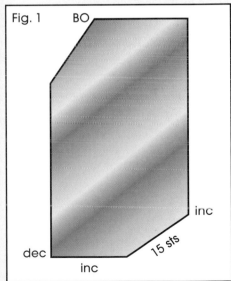

Fig. 1
BO
dec
inc
15 sts
inc

5. Refer to Technique 3, Knit 2 together on page 51. Cont in patt, and AT THE SAME TIME, inc in the 1st st and dec by k2tog on the last 2 sts of

yarn and beg working Color Pattern at Row 5. Cont working patt, changing yarns as indicated, and carrying yarn as you go:

Color Pattern:

· <u>Rows 1–2:</u> K with worsted-weight yarn.
<u>Rows 3–4:</u> K with 1st bulky-weight yarn.
<u>Rows 5–6:</u> K with worsted-weight yarn.
<u>Rows 7–8:</u> K with 2nd bulky-weight yarn.

every other row until the height of increase (higher) side measures 22" (24", 24", 24"). This will maintain the same number of stitches—or the number you noted in Step 4—per row.

6. Beg dec by k2tog at each end of every other row until shoulder (top horizontal measurement under needles) measures 5½" (6½", 7½", 8"). (There should be approximately 25 rem on medium.) BO all sts loosely.

Knitting the Right Back

7. With 1st bulky-weight yarn, CO 3 sts. K 1 row. Change to worsted-weight yarn and beg working Color Pattern at Row 5. AT THE SAME TIME, inc in the 1st and last stitch of this row and every other row, working patt and changing yarns until you reach the same number noted in Step 4 for left front.

8. Repeat Step 5.

9. Beg dec by k2tog at each end of every other row until there are 3 rem. BO all sts loosely.

Knitting the Left Back

10. Repeat Step 7.

11. Cont in patt, and AT THE SAME TIME, dec by k2tog in the 1st 2 sts and inc in the last st of every other row until the height of increase (higher) side measures 22" (24", 24", 24").

12. Repeat Step 9.

Knitting the Sleeves

13. With 1st bulky-weight yarn, CO 30 (34, 34, 34) sts. K 1 row. Change to worsted-weight yarn and beg working Color Pattern at Row 5. AT THE SAME TIME, inc in the 1st and last stitch of this row and every other row four times, then every 4 rows 11 (13, 13, 14) times to equal 60 (68, 68, 70) sts until piece measures 17" (17½") or desired sleeve length. BO all sts. Repeat for second sleeve.

Note: Before binding off, you may wish to put sleeves on stitch holder or a circular needle and adjust the sleeve length after you sew shoulders and back seam of garment. Pin sleeve to shoulder and under arm of jacket to determine appropriate length. Then add to the length as needed, continuing in the Color Pattern.

Knitting the Front-closure Tabs

14. With 1st bulky-weight yarn, CO 30 sts. BO these same sts loosely. Repeat for four tabs.

Knitting the Back Belt Tab

15. With 1st bulky-weight yarn CO 7 sts. Work in garter stitch until piece measures 5½". BO all sts loosely.

Finishing the Jacket

16. Refer to Blocking on page 32. Block all pieces to specified measurements.

17. Refer to Assembling/Sewing Seams on pages 32–36. With a tapestry needle and worsted-weight yarn, sew shoulder seams 5½" (6½", 7½", 8") from armholes.

18. Arrange right and left back pieces so they form an upside down "V." Sew back pieces together, leaving a 5½" (7½") slit at bottom.

19. Set in sleeves by folding in half. Match the midpoint to shoulder seam. Pin to armhole with a safety pin. Sew sleeves and side seams.

20. Tack down fold-over collar.

21. Place belt tab above back slit and tack down. Sew buttons onto each side of tab. (See Photo A)

22. With crochet hook and worsted-weight yarn, slip-stitch crochet across back neck as necessary to stabilize. Crochet up fronts of jacket.

Photo A

Slip-stitch Crochet

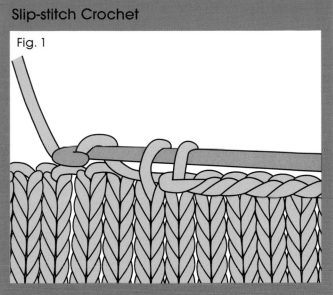

Fig. 1

a. With the yarn at the WS of the work, insert the crochet hook between two stitches from front to back and pull the yarn through to the front, creating a loop. Keeping loop on crochet hook, move forward one or two rows, and insert crochet hook through new stitch as before. Pull the yarn through to the front and through the previous loop, creating a new loop on the crochet hook. Repeat. (See Fig. 1)

FYI—The names given to the garter stitch and the stockinette stitch date back to the days when stockings were knitted by hand. The stockinette stitch, or stocking stitch as the English call it, was used to make up the lower fitted portion of the stocking that fit over the foot and calf. Since the garter stitch had more give to it, it was customarily used for the upper section of the stocking that had to fit over the thigh.

23. Place front closure tabs approximately 5½" and 7½" (7½" and 10½") from bottom of left and right front. Separately thread each yarn tail onto a tapestry needle, pull through to WS of piece, and tie in a square knot. Trim ends.

24. Refer to Weaving in Yarn Ends & Tails on page 31. Weave in all ends.

Tips

The runs of color in each skein of yarn used for this sample are quite long. The colorway of olive/taupe/chartreuse had one run of plum/lavender in each skein of each quality of yarn. Each piece was started with a new skein of yarn and the plums in each skein generally lined up.

Finished garment bust measurements for this pattern range from 36" to 48". If you wish to make the jacket smaller or larger, adjust the number of stitches on the three diagonal panels. If the gauge is correct, simply increase or decrease each piece by 7 stitches to make your garment 8" larger or smaller. You will also need to make the same adjustment to the right front that is knit horizontally.

How do I add beads into my knitting?

Double-pointed knitting
  needles: Size 0000
  (1.25mm), set of 3
Knitting needles:
  Size 0000 (1.25mm)
Perle cotton thread:
  #8, 10 gm: pale green,
  1 ball
Seed beads: Size 11, green iris,
  1 hank

There are two main techniques for knitting with beads: Beaded Knitting and Bead Knitting. Both forms of knitting with beads were popular throughout the 18th century and the first part of the 19th century. Items such as bags, scarves, dresses, mittens, gloves, and lace were all decorated using both methods.

This project uses the "Beaded Knitting" method. This is a fairly simple technique, requiring the ability to cast on, do a basic knit stitch, and bind off. During the knitting process, beads are slid into place between stitches with the bead hole lying parallel to the needle. The knitting yarn or thread is visible as part of the finished product.

Window Pane Beaded Pendant Bag

Designed by Theresa Williams

Skill level: intermediate

Finished measurements: 2" x 2½"

Notes: The size 0000 (1.25mm) knitting needles can be difficult to find. Check with your local knitting shop.

We recommend that you purchase seed beads in a hank to save time and sanity. A hank of seed beads consists of a bundle of individual strands of strung beads. If you choose to use seed beads that are not prestrung on hanks, be aware that you will have to string each bead individually onto the perle cotton prior to knitting the project. Seed beads are commonly available at bead shops, local craft stores, or several sources through mail order.

Here's how:

Notes: Knitting with perle cotton thread feels different than knitting with a more commonly used weight yarn. At first it may feel as though there is nothing to hang onto, since the perle cotton is so thin. The first row is the most difficult—once you have completed it, you will find that the rest of the project is relatively simple.

During knitting, you will slide or slip the indicated number of seed beads into place against the previous knit stitch prior to knitting the next stitch. The knitting locks them into place. The beads appear on the underside of each row as it is knitted, ensuring that the beads will appear on both the inside and outside of the bag.

This project is knitted in one piece, starting at the top and then working down the front, across the bottom and up over the back side.

Gauge is not important.

Transferring the Beads onto the Perle Cotton

1. Transfer a portion of the seed beads—three strands at a time—onto the ball of perle cotton prior to beginning the knitting.

Transfer Beads onto Perle Cotton

a.   Break one end of one strand of beads from your hank and tie a large knot in it. Break the other end of the strand from the hank so that it is free.

b.   Fold the free end of the thread over onto itself forming a loop. Make an overhand knot to hold this loop in place. (See Fig. 1) If there is not enough thread exposed to make the knot, remove a few beads until there is enough room. You will have made the bead strand into a "string needle" having an eye at one end.

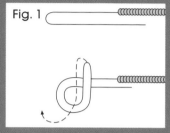
Fig. 1

c.   Thread the loose end of your perle cotton through the eye of your "string needle," leaving a tail of at least 8". (See Fig. 2)

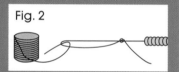
Fig. 2

d.   Carefully slide the beads over the knot and onto the perle cotton. If a bead refuses to slide over onto the perle cotton, unthread your string needle, remove the bead, and start the process again.

Notes: It is not essential to transfer all of the beads to the perle cotton before beginnng to knit. In doing a small amount at a time, the perle cotton gets less wear from the process of sliding the beads along it while knitting.

When you have knitted in all or nearly all of the beads that you transferred onto the perle cotton, complete the row that you are working on, break the thread, and add more beads. Avoid trying to add beads in the middle of a row as it can make the bag look untidy.

Watch for and remove any irregular-shaped or odd-colored beads.

Knitting the Bag

2.   Refer to Technique 1, Cast On on page 41. With knitting needles, CO 23 sts.

3.   Refer to Technique 1, Knit on page 42. Work as follows:

Rows 1–2: K23.
Rows 3–4: K2, [slip 1 bead, k1] 20 times, k1.
Rows 5–6: K2, [slip 1 bead, k1] two times, [slip 2 beads, k1, slip 1 bead, k1, slip 1 bead, k1] six times, k1.
Rows 7–12: K4, [slip 2 beads, k3] five times, slip 2 beads, k4.
Rows 13–16: Rep rows 5–6 two times.
Rows 17–22: Rep rows 7–12 one time.
Rows 23–26: Rep rows 5–6 two times.
Rows 27–32: Rep rows 7–12 one time.
Rows 33–36: Rep rows 5–6 two times.
Rows 37–42: Rep rows 7–12 one time.
Rows 43–46: Rep rows 5–6 two times.
Row 47: K3, [slip 1 bead, k2] 10 times.
Rows 48–49: K2, [slip 1 bead, k2] nine times, slip 1 bead, k3.
Rows 50–51: Rep row 47 two times.
Rows 52–53: Rep rows 48–49 one time.
Rows 54–55: Rep row 47 two times.
Rows 56–57: Rep rows 48–49 one time.
Rows 58–59: Rep row 47 two times.
Row 60: Rep row 48 one time.
Row 61: [K2, slip 30 beads] 10 times, k3.
Row 62: K23.
Row 63: Rep row 48 one time.
Rows 64–65: Rep row 47 two times.
Rows 66–67: Rep rows 48–49 one time.
Rows 68–69: Rep row 47 two times.
Rows 70–71: Rep rows 48–49 one time.
Rows 72–73: Rep row 47 two times.
Rows 74–75: Rep rows 48–49 one time.
Row 76: Rep row 47 one time.
Rows 77–80: Rep rows 5–6 two times.
Rows 81–86: Rep rows 7–12 one time.
Rows 87–90: Rep rows 5–6 two times.
Rows 91–96: Rep rows 7–12 one time.

Rows 97–100: Rep rows 5–6 two times.
Rows 101–106: Rep rows 7–12 one time.
Rows 107–110: Rep rows 5–6 two times.
Rows 111–116: Rep rows 7–12 one time.
Rows 117–128: Rep rows 5–6 six times.
Rows 129–134: Rep rows 7–12 one time.
Rows 135–138: Rep rows 5–6 two times.
Row 139: BO 4 sts, k2, [slip 2 beads, k3] four times, k4.
Row 140: BO 4 sts, k2, [slip 2 beads, k3] four times.
Row 141–144: [K3, slip 2 beads] four times, k3.
Rows 145–148: [K1, slip 1 bead] two times, [slip 2 beads, k1, slip 1 bead, k1, slip 1 bead, k1] four times.
Row 149: BO 2 sts, [slip 2 beads, k3] four times.
Row 150: BO 2 sts, [slip 2 beads, k3] three times, slip 2 beads, k1.
Rows 151–154: K1, [slip 2 beads, k3] three times, slip 2 beads, k1.
Rows 155–158: [K1, slip 1 bead] 10 times, k1.

4. Refer to Technique 1, Bind Off on page 43. BO all sts.

Making a Knitted Cord

5. With double-pointed needles, CO 6 sts. Make a slip cord. BO all sts.

Make a Slip Cord	Fig. 1

a. Knit 1 row.

b. Without turning the work, slide the stitches to the right end of needle. Pull thread to tighten. (See Fig. 1)

c. Repeat a–b until desired length.

Finishing the Bag

6. Refer to Assembling/Sewing Seams on pages 32–36. Fold the bag in half with right sides together, so that the beaded fringe (Row 61) is along the bottom edge inside of the bag. With tapestry needle, sew the side seams.

7. Refer to Weaving in Yarn Ends & Tails on page 31. Weave in all ends.

8. Turn the bag right side out.

9. Refer to Blocking on page 32. If necessary, block the bag.

10. Sew one end of finished cord onto upper edge of each side seam.

Tips

Try experimenting with different-sized perle cotton threads, different-sized beads, and different-sized knitting needles.

Look for contrast when selecting beads and perle cotton so the beads do not blend into the knitting.

Theresa Williams is cofounder and the creative energy behind BagLady Press. She has authored the company's Beaded Bag Series of books and has designed many of the fabric bag designs used with the BagLady purse frame line. She has written articles on beaded knitting for both *Interweave Knits* magazine and *McCall's Needlework* magazine.

BagLady Press offers books on beaded knitted bags, bead crochet bags, beaded bag kits, hard to-find knitting needles (sizes 00 through 000000), seed beads and the complete Presencia/Finca line of perle cotton, crochet cotton, sewing and embroidery threads and other supplies.

8
project

What you need to get started:

Circular knitting needles:
    Size 10 (6mm)
Double-pointed knitting
    needles: Size 10 (6mm)
Yarn:
    100% wool: red, 2 skeins

How do I felt a knitted piece?

Felting is a process of matting and shrinking (called fulling) a project made of 100% wool by exposing the yarn to warm or hot water. The shrinkage differs from yarn to yarn and as a direct result of the water temperature. Soap is added to the process to help make the yarn oily and to "unlock" the wool fibers during washing. As the yarn cools and dries, the fibers tangle, or lock, into the sturdy material we recognize as felt.

Felted Stocking

Stitched by Penny Toliver for the Vanessa-Ann Collection

Skill level: intermediate

Finished measurements: Before felting: 9½" x 29".
After felting: 7" x 17". (See Photo A)

Here's how:

Knitting the Stocking

1. Knit a stocking that is half again the size desired after felting.

Machine Felting

2. Place the piece in a mesh bag or nylon stocking depending on the size of the piece.

3. Set your washing machine for warm water, low-water level, and gentle cycle.

4. Add regular laundry soap and proceed through the agitation cycle.

   Note: Adding other garments will help in the felting, as the friction of the garments aids the process.

5. Repeat Steps 3–4 as needed to obtain the desired shrinkage. Check the project often.

   Note: Sometimes it takes several washing cycles to felt the project to the size you desire.

6. When the piece is the desired size, spin, rinse and spin, then remove it from the machine.

7. Dry in a warm dryer and steam-press the piece on a towel to form.

Notes: Tepid water is the best way to control the amount of shrinkage. This process is irreversible as the water temperature causes the wool fibers to become tangled so that they will not return to their original shape.

Machine washable yarn should not be used for felting.

There are many interesting projects that can be made using this technique; some of which are picture mats, hot pads, coasters, tote bags, slippers, mittens, hats, golf club covers, Christmas decorations, balls, and even pin cushions.

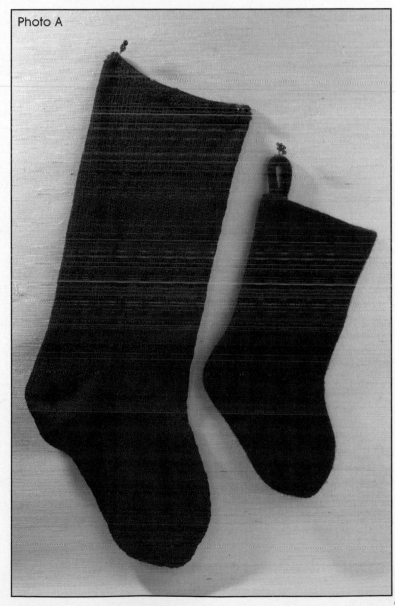

Photo A

designed by Colinette Yarns, Ltd.

designed by Mission Falls

designed by Mission Falls

designed by Andrea and Gayle Shackleton

designed by Andrea and Gayle Shackleton

Section 4: the gallery

designed by Leanne Bennette

designed by Colinette Yarns, Ltd.

In 1982, **Anne Maillette** and her family moved to the Wisconsin Northwoods to enjoy a simpler life. However, the months of winter posed a challenge for Anne in keeping her family warm. In response, Anne began to knit wool sweaters and accessories which enabled her husband and three girls to call winter their favorite season.

What began as a hobby became a cottage industry, and in 1988, Annie's Woolens was established.

designed by Anne Maillette

designed by Anne Maillette

designed by Anne Maillette

designed by Anne Maillette

Leanne Bennett's first knitting project was in the second grade in Los Angeles when her mother taught her how to knit diaper covers for her teacher's new baby. Since then, she has knit everything from suits to socks, knit for and taught family and friends how to knit, has had a small knitting business, and has sold her hand-knits at craft fairs to ski lodges. Now she prefers small portable projects like hats, gloves, scarves, and socks because they work up faster. Besides knitting, Leanne practices Yoga and sells real estate in Salt Lake City, Utah, where she resides. She spends much of her summertime knitting and quilting in her 100-year-old mountain cabin.

designed by Leanne Bennett

designed by Leanne Bennett

designed by Leanne Bennett

designed by Mission Falls

designed by Mission Falls

104

designed by Mission Falls

Mission Falls is a mythical knitters' paradise on the shores of Lake Ontario. However, there is nothing mythical about Mission Falls' wonderful natural fiber yarns and pattern books.

Established in 1992, Mission Falls rapidly became known in Canada as a purveyor of wonderful yarns and distinct knit design.

In 1999, they launched the first of their "1824" line of yarns to an international knitting audience. Mission Falls 1824 Wool is true Aran weight yarn with an incredibly soft hand. Mission Falls is distributed by Unique Kolours, Ltd.

designed by Mission Falls

designed by Colinette Yarns, Ltd.

Colinette Yarns, Ltd. was founded by Colinette Sansbury and her husband Geoff over 15 years ago when Colinette, a textile designer, could not find appropriate fabrics for her work. Geoff, a *Prix di Roma* oil painter, began dying yarns that Colinette could use for creating her designs. People quickly began asking them for the yarns from which the garments were created, so the business' focus began to change from making finished garments to dying yarn for consumers to knit. That was the birth of Colinette Yarns.

Over time, the business grew from carrying only a few yarns and colors to a wide range of yarns and over 100 colors. Though the size of their operation has changed, the yarns are still dyed the old-fashioned way, one bag at a time.

Today, Colinette Yarns is one of the largest hand-dyed yarn suppliers in the world, with distributors in Canada, England, Germany, Sweden, and the U.S. Colinette Yarns, Ltd., is distributed by Unique Kolours, Ltd.

designed by Colinette Yarns, Ltd.

designed by Colinette Yarns, Ltd.

designed by Colinette Yarns, Ltd.

designed by Andrea and Gayle Shackleton

Fifteen years ago, Andrea and Gayle Shackleton, two sisters from Northern California, started designing and knitting sweaters by hand. With love of fine art, heirloom knitting, crochet, antique buttons, and trims, they created one-of-a-kind pieces for private collections and galleries. Andrea and Gayle now design both Hot Knots and Tara sweaters. Their lines also include fine dresses, accessories, and children's sweaters.

At home in Arcata, California, where **Hot Knots** is based, they have a small group of talented women, working together to create fine pieces of wearable art. In the last year, they have opened a store in this little gold-rush town. Arcata has been a great new source of creativity and inspiration.

In 1990, ATA (Aid to Artisans) asked them to help out with a women's knitting cooperative in Nepal. More than 10 years later, Andrea and Gayle are lucky enough to still work with the wonderful women of ACP (Association of Craft Producers). The Tara sweaters are hand-knit by ACP, a nonprofit women's cooperative in Kathmandu, Nepal. ACP dyes all of the yarn for Tara sweaters with technology that is clean and nonpolluting. Being given the opportunity to work with ACP has been one of the richest experiences of their lives. Named for the Nepali Goddess of compassion, Tara represents their ever expanding collaboration.

designed by Andrea and Gayle Shackleton

Photo by Robin Robin

designed by Andrea and Gayle Shackleton

Photo by Robin Robin

109

Yarn Information & Acknowledgments

The following is a complete list of the yarns used for each project pictured in the book. Visit your local yarn shop to obtain the yarn shown or to find a similar yarn.

Technique 1
Square Kitchen Cloths, Page 40
100% mercerized cotton; 2 oz ball: 1 Red, 1 Red/Black

Technique 2
Toddler Cardigan, Page 44
Mission Falls 1824 Cotton (100% cotton; 84 yds [77m]/50 gm ball):
6 Fog #400, 1 Chicory #401

Technique 3
Child's Cardigan, Page 48
GGH Boboli (100% nylon microfiber; 88 yds [80m]/50 gm ball): 4 (4, 5) Slate Blue #18

Technique 4
Child's Shell, Page 53
GGH Samoa (50% cotton, 50% acrylic microfiber; 104.5 yds [95m]/50 gm ball): 3 (3, 4) Slate Blue #84

Technique 5
Baby Booties, Page 57
Mission Falls 1824 Cotton (100% cotton; 84 yds [77m]/50 gm ball):
1 Fog #400
1 Chicory #401

Technique 6
Stars & Stripes Baby Sweater, Page 59
Karabella Aurora 8 (100% machine-washable merino wool; 98 yds/50 gm skein): 2 (3) Sand #1360, 2 Wine #0002, 1 Midnight #0001

Technique 7
Stars & Stripes Baby Hat, Page 65
Karabella Aurora 8 (100% machine-washable merino wool; 98 yds/50 gm skein): 2 (3) Sand #1360, 2 Wine #0002, 1 Midnight #0001

Technique 8
Yipes! Stripes! Cardigan, Page 68
Muench's Tessin (43% wool, 35% acrylic, 22% cotton machine-washable; 110 yds/100 gm skein): 2 Red (MC) #65805, 1 Yellow (CC) #65839

Technique 9
Moose Christmas Stocking, Page 72
Bartletteyarns 2-ply worsted wool (100% worsted wool; 210 yds/100 gm [4 oz] skein): 1 Spruce Heather, 1 Light Sheep Grey, 1 Cranberry

Project 1
Simple Embellishments, Page 80
Rowan Wool Cotton (50% wool, 50% cotton; 123 yds [113m]/50 gm skein): 1 Flower #943

Project 2
Bassinet Blanket, Page 82
Bernat Softee Baby (100% acrylic; 140 gm [5 oz] skein): 1 Pale Blue

Project 3
Eyeleted Baby Hat, Page 84
Mission Falls 1824 Cotton (100% cotton; 84 yds [77m]/50 gm ball):
1 Chicory #401

Project 4
Pumpkin Ornament, Page 86
2-ply worsted wool yarn: 1 orange

Project 5
Mini Sweater, Page 88
2-ply worsted wool yarn: 1 red/blue tweed

Project 6
Origami Jacket, Page 90
Noro Silk Garden (45% silk, 45% kid mohair, 10% lamb's wool; 110 yds [100m]/50 gm skein): 5 (5, 6, 6) Olive #34

Noro Implessions (43% kid mohair, 32% lamb's wool, 20% silk, 5% nylon; 60 yds [48m]/40 gm skein): 5 (5, 6, 6) Olive #4 (2nd (hairy) bulky weight yarn)
Noro Yamabuki (43% kid mohair, 32% lamb's wool, 20% silk, 5% nylon; 60 yds [48m]/40 gm skein): 5 (5, 6, 6) Olive #4 (1st (bouclé) bulky weight yarn)

Project 7
Window Pane Beaded Pendant Bag, Page 94
#8 perle cotton (10 gm ball): 1 Finca #4799
Size 11 seed beads (hank): 1 Green Iris

Annie's Woolens
Anne Mailette
1668 Watersmeet Lake Road
Eagle River, WI 54521
T: 1-715-479-7185
www.annieswoolens.com
e-mail: anniwool@newnorth.net

Bag Lady Press
Theresa Williams
PO Box 2409
Evergreen, CO 80437
T: 1-888-222-4523
F: 1-303-670-2179
www.baglady.com
e-mail: baglady@baglady.com

Karen Baumer
Los Angeles, California

Knitted Threads Designs, LLC
Janet Rehfeldt
1857 Frawley Drive
Sun Prairie, WI 53590
www.knittedthreads.com

Song Palmese
Oakland, California

Unique Kolours Ltd.
www.uniquekolours.com

Wooly Knits Yarn Shop
Donna Barnako
6728 Lowell Avenue
McLean, VA 22102
T: 1-703-759-3549
e-mail: Donna@WoolyKnits.com

Bibliography of Books

Knitting for Dummies, by Pam Allen, 2002, Hungry Minds, Inc., New York

The Handknitter's Handbook, by Montse Stanley, 1990, Sterling Publishing Co. Inc., New York

Big Book of Knitting, by Katharina Buss, 2001, Sterling Publishing Co. Inc., New York

The Good Housekeeping Illustrated Book of Needlecrafts, Cecelia K. Toth, 1994, Carroll & Brown Limited and The Hearst Corporation, New York

Metric Equivalency Chart

inches to millimetres and centimetres (mm-millimetres   cm-centimetres)

inches	mm	cm	inches	cm	inches	cm	inches	cm
⅛	3	0.3	6	15.2	21	53.3	36	91.4
¼	6	0.6	7	17.8	22	55.9	37	94.0
⅜	10	1.0	8	20.3	23	58.4	38	96.5
½	13	1.3	9	22.9	24	61.0	39	99.1
⅝	16	1.6	10	25.4	25	63.5	40	101.6
¾	19	1.9	11	27.9	26	66.0	41	104.1
⅞	22	2.2	12	30.5	27	68.6	42	106.7
1	25	2.5	13	33.0	28	71.1	43	109.2
1¼	32	3.2	14	35.6	29	73.7	44	111.8
1½	38	3.8	15	38.1	30	76.2	45	114.3
1¾	44	4.4	16	40.6	31	78.7	46	116.8
2	51	5.1	17	43.2	32	81.3	47	119.4
3	76	7.6	18	45.7	33	83.8	48	121.9
4	102	10.2	19	48.3	34	86.4	49	124.5
5	127	12.7	20	50.8	35	88.9	50	127.0

Index